Raisin' Brains:

Surviving My Smart Family

Karen L. J. Isaacson

Great Potential Press, Inc.
Scottsdale, AZ
www.giftedbooks.com

Raisin' Brains: Surviving My Smart Family
Cover Design and Interior Illustrations: Hutchison-Frey
Interior Design: The Printed Page

Published by
Great Potential Press, Inc.
P.O. Box 5057
Scottsdale, AZ 85261
© 2002 by Great Potential Press, Inc.
Printed and bound in the United States of America
09 08 07   5 4 3 2

Library of Congress Cataloging-in-Publication Data

Isaacson, Karen L. J., 1965-
  Raisin' brains : surviving my smart family / Karen L. J. Isaacson.
    p. cm.
  ISBN 0-910707-54-5
  1. Family life--Humor. 2. Gifted children--Humor. I. Title.
PN6231.F3 I82 2002
814'.6--dc21
                              2002010653

# Dedication

*I would like to dedicate this book to my husband
and my five incredibly awesome children.
I love you guys!*

Preface

I have always felt a little out of place in this world and wondered if other people—at least some of them—didn't feel the same way. I think I've spent my life playing "Concentration." I keep turning over different people cards hoping to find a friend that matches me, hoping to find another connection to the world. Most of the time I find at least one or two similarities on every card, especially when I take the time to examine the card closely. It is rare when I find a card similar to mine, and the only near-perfect matches I've ever found have been close family members. I value those connections, those matches, because we speak the same language. It's as though I'm lost in a big city and someone else comes along who is just as lost as I am, but somehow, just hanging out with her is enough to help me find my bearings and give me the confidence to tackle what, moments before, seemed impossible.

We live in a society built on peer pressure—sometimes good, sometimes not so good. But the pressure to fit in and to belong and to be normal can be as overwhelming as a big city is to a small-town hick like me. Sometimes, when people try too hard to fit into a mold, they get lost in a world that doesn't belong to them. In writing this book, I wanted to reach out to those who grew up feeling different, maybe even a little weird.

Some of you probably had really strange parents, and you were afraid they'd show up at school one day and frighten away your hard-earned friends. Some of you probably have really strange kids and wonder if that's okay and if they're going to survive; and then you wonder if maybe you really were abducted by aliens during your pregnancy and later gave birth to their offspring, even though your offspring appear to be human, at least on the surface.

Some of you are probably strange at heart, but keep it well hidden. You know who you are. You're the ones who turn the radio on and shake your bootie in front of the mirror in the privacy of your own home, but would die a thousand deaths before you'd tap your toes in public. Then there are those of you who are just you. You might be strange without even realizing it.

Perhaps I'm wrong, but my theory is that most people, no matter how normal they may appear to be, have been affected by strange and unique people at some point in their lives. And so when I play the game of "People Concentration," there may be few perfect matches, but there are always enough similarities to keep the game interesting. It is my hope that those common experiences will be a connection as readers see bits and pieces of themselves or their friends and families in this book, and that they will laugh with relief to know there are others out there like them.

Another reason I wrote this book was that I hoped to give the readers some insight as to what the term "gifted" really means. It's an often-misunderstood term. I mean, sure, technically it implies that a person displays exceptional potential in a given area. But what does it mean in real, everyday life? The short answer to that question is a sinister laugh, "Buwahahaha!" The long answer is at least partially attempted in this book.

The final reason that I wrote this book was because I couldn't help it. All my life, these stories have been collecting and waiting for an audience with a sympathetic ear. Ever since I first realized how terribly picked on I was by my mother and father, who only brought me into this world so that they could have someone to embarrass and torment, I have been looking for an opportunity to tell the world the true story of life at our house. This, then, is my message in a bottle, and I'm dropping it into the big ocean of humanity knowing that somewhere, some reader is going to pick it up and say, "Hey! This could be me! A perfect match!"

This is also a message on behalf of my children, who are also terribly picked on and have been blessed with an equally embarrassing and tormenting set of parents. The tradition lives on!

> *Please note: The names of the characters in this book have been changed to more accurately fit their personalities and to protect the not-so-innocent. Besides, their real names are boring.*

Acknowledgments

I would like to express gratitude to my husband and children for their love and support and willingness to go without hot meals; to my siblings for their friendship and their laughter; to my parents for their patience and wisdom; and to my grandmother, Dula, for her strength, her individuality, and her ability to make something beautiful out of nothing at all. I would also like to thank Charles Hackenberry, Debra Seabury, and Patricia Cox for their friendship and writing advice, and my editor, Janet Gore, for her cheerfulness, encouragement, and most of all, for her editing. Oh, and I need to thank all of those wonderful friends who have contributed their experience to or their enthusiasm for this project, as well as all of those who have gone out of their way to contribute to the education of my children. Thank you!

McGillicuddy Family Tree

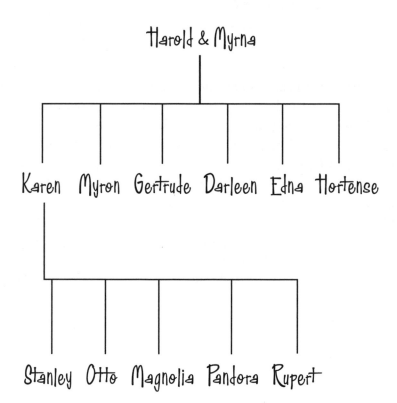

Harold & Myrna

Karen Myron Gertrude Darleen Edna Hortense

Stanley Otto Magnolia Pandora Rupert

Contents

Dedication. iii

Preface v

Acknowledgments ix

Family Tree x

Chapter 1: Are You My Mother? 1

Chapter 2: What Do You Mean, He's Reading? 17

Chapter 3: School Days, School Days. 29

Chapter 4: Just So I Win 35

Chapter 5: For the Love of Mummies. 49

Chapter 6: Hocus, Focus 59

Chapter 7: It's Only a Test 79

Chapter 8: Can You Repeat the Question? 91

Chapter 9: I Already Know How 109

Chapter 10: I Gotta Be Me 123

Chapter 11: Brain Food 135

Chapter 12: Two for the Show. 143

Chapter 13: Great Expectations 163

Chapter 14: Weird Can Be Beautiful 173

About the Author 184

1: Are You My Mother?

My first introduction to a "gifted and talented" person was at birth—my birth. The details surrounding that moment are a bit fuzzy in my mind, but I'm sure my mother must have been exhibiting telltale signs all along.

Fortunately, my little child brain was able to gradually take her strangeness in.

I am the recovering child of a gifted parent.

I was always confused about my mom. I suppose I felt a mixture of pride, because she was different from everyone else's mom, and embarrassment, because she was different from everyone else's mom.

My first clue that something was amiss was when I entered a public school building for the first time. It was first grade. I missed kindergarten because we lived out in The Boonies. A wonderful place, The Boonies. It was only seven miles away from town, but those seven miles were thick with trees and mountains that stood as a barrier between us and the civilized world—especially as my mother couldn't drive me there. Kindergarten was only a half day, and while the bus came every morning and afternoon, my mom was unable to transport me in between times, so I remained at home, blissfully ignorant.

In The Boonies, we were allowed to grow up free from conventions—such as matching clothing that was worn right-side out, and the pressures of fitting in with our peers, or even realizing that we had any. That is, unless you want to count the farm animals, which included a lamb named Lamby (very original, I know) and a pig named Arnold, (after a good friend of ours), as well as numerous other quadrupeds and egg-laying creatures. The egg-laying creatures were my favorites. They weren't big enough to scare me, and they were fun to catch, but the highlight of their existence, in our humble opinion, was when it was their time to go to the Great Chicken Coop in the Sky. We kids would sit down in the bleacher section of the barnyard, and my dad would, with great showmanship and much skill, chop off the chicken's head.

It was like *Alice in Wonderland* meets *A Tale of Two Cities* meets *The Headless Horseman*, because after the chicken lost its head, it would then, to our delight and amazement, proceed to squawk and do the Funky Chicken in circles across the straw. That was in the good old days, before all of the violence on TV.

You've heard of *A Chicken Every Sunday*? Well, at our house, it was a chicken every Saturday night, live at the coop, no charge for admission.

We lived in an old, white, two-story farmhouse with a wood stove and a black and white checkered floor in the kitchen. We also had a regular, boring stove, and an indoor sink with running water, but other than indoor plumbing and a TV with one fuzzy channel on a good day, that was the extent of our modern conveniences.

That farmhouse and the surrounding acres were the beginnings of memory for me. My whole life took place there, it seems, except for Sundays, when we went to church. Even church has farmhouse associations with it, as I recall my mom being late for church and getting locked out of the house with pink foam curlers still in her hair. My brother and I were in awe when she kicked the back door down. Sure, it may have been an old door, and it didn't take much to do it in, but the act was so out of character for my mom that we were impressed and really rather proud of her.

2

That place may have been my world, but it was a wide one. We had over a hundred acres of pasture, forest, and pond. The pond was a lovely place to swim after the muddy sludge settled. The mud was great for mud pies. We always went into the water cleaner than we were when we came out of it. Thankfully, my mom was not uptight about dirty clothes. She understood, as she spent most of her outdoor time in one of her two huge gardens.

Frogs loved our pond, too. When my mom's younger sister was a teenager, she came to live with us for the summer. She loved frogs, cooked with a little salt and pepper. She used to sit on pontoons and float in the middle of the pond and eat frog legs to her heart's content.

Ah, the good life.

The Boonies—it was a magical place full of enchantment, where frog legs are a delicacy, where chickens give Oscar-worthy performances, and the only place I know where you have the luxury of sledding down a snowy white hillside and landing in a soft, warm pile of manure.

Like Alice through the looking glass, these were the halcyon days of my preschool life. And I was supposed to know how to fit in to a regular classroom full of civilized people when I went to first grade? I mean, I'd never even heard of paste before. How backwards was that?

I was also naively unaware of important little things like the alphabet. I remember my mother sitting down with me a few days before I began first grade: "Let's go over it one more time. A, B, C, D...."

Cramming for first grade. In all my six years, I had never heard of the alphabet. She'd tried to explain the solar system to me, but the alphabet? Uh huh. She said she didn't set out to teach me anything, but she did her best to answer my many questions. Silly me. I didn't know enough to ask about the alphabet.

I was excited about school, even though at least every other day I was on the bus and nearly to school before I realized that my dress was inside out. One of the first lessons I learned during first grade was that it's wise to turn on the lights when you get dressed and to check to see which side of your clothing the seams are on. Then there was the ponytail problem. My mom used to fix my hair by grabbing a handful of hair on either side of my head and then securing each handful with a rubber band. It's much faster than going to all of the effort of dividing the hair evenly, and parting it down the middle. I felt as though I were an alien from the planet Carbuncle. My only role models up to that point, other than my parents, relatives, and a few friends of the family, had been the Flintstones. I did see other kids now and then when friends of our family stopped by to visit, but it was never in a socially pressured atmosphere.

Now that I think back, I *did* have a boyfriend during my preschool years. His name was Sinbad the Sailor. But sadly, it was a one-sided affair. That animated, early morning TV hunk with big eyes and a perfect tan never knew I existed.

"School" was a big brick building with twenty-four class-rooms, first through sixth grade. The school was big enough to put a kid like me in awe, but I don't remember being scared when my mom dropped me off. It was instead a matter of curiosity. There I was on a new planet, and I was eager to boldly go where I had never gone before. I remember the feeling that I had the first time I sat at my wooden desk. It was an official sort of feeling, as though I had finally become part of the human race. The desk clinched it. I looked around at the other twenty-five first graders and was sure they felt the same way I did. I might as well have had "novice" tattooed over my eyebrows. I sat there with a silly grin, thrilled to have discovered the place.

I ate up the business of reading. Sally, Dick, Jane, and Spot opened up a whole new world for me. Granted, it was a world made up of repetitive one-syllable words, and nobody did any-thing more exciting than look or run. Still, I knew the potential was there, and I yearned to explore it. It wasn't long before I found the *Little House on the Prairie* series and began sneaking books into bed at night for a little covert reading.

Math, on the other hand, was really quite pointless. As far as I was concerned, it was nothing more than an unfathomable mess of chicken scratch symbols.

I was well behaved. My mother said she never had to spank me; all she had to do was look at me wrong and I would start crying. I tell you this because it's important that you believe that I did *not* steal those lunch tickets in first grade. I was framed, and I know who did do it. It was Lance. Apparently he'd forgotten his lunch money, and his digestive juices began to attack his brain and threaten an overthrow if he didn't come up with some grub that day. He stole those tickets from another girl, Linda. Then, when he was afraid he'd be found out, he ditched them in my desk. Why my desk? Probably because it was conveniently located and conveniently messy enough. Everything else was stashed in there—why not a couple of lunch tickets too? So when the teacher (with Lance's help) found the lunch tickets in my possession, she had no other alternative but to give me a hack.

I'd seen kids get hacks before—boys anyway—and they all did the same thing. They ran around the room screaming and hurling desks into the teacher's path until she finally grabbed them by the scruff of the neck and hacked their hiney-hoos a good one. So having no other example to follow, what did I do when it was my turn? I screamed, ran around the room, and hurled desks. I thought it was protocol. Of course, afterwards, I sat at my desk, hung my head, and cried pathetically from the shame of it all.

At recess, we had two choices: we could play kissy-tag or jump rope. Kissy-tag wasn't any fun, because the cute boys never chased me. And I'd never seen a jump rope before in my life. When I finally did see one that first day on the playground, I didn't know what all of the other girls were so excited about. It sure didn't look like much to me.

I was a social vacuum waiting to be filled with the examples of my peers. Everyone else knew some secret that I didn't. The secret was called "fitting in," a.k.a. being "normal." I observed and copied as well as I could, but in all my years of public schooling, I never felt as though I belonged there with everyone else.

Now I know why.

I blame it on my mother. Perhaps it was the pea bread that she invented just in time to serve at a party. Picture banana bread, except when you slice it, you find a treasure trove of slimy, peely, smashed legumes, formerly known as canned peas. It's delicious with jam. Lots and lots of jam.

Maybe I could blame it on the brown bag lunches that my mom decorated for me when I was in high school—the ones that had "Little Karen McGillicuddy" written over the smiley-faced stick figures—all done in an eye-catching wide-tipped black marker. Maybe I could pin it on the fact that she let my sisters push her around in a grocery cart at the supermarket, or that she sang and danced around the living room. We kept the drapes closed since we had moved into town by that time and had neighbors. Imagine a middle-aged mother of six wearing eye-blinding bubblegum pink leotards and doing dramatic dance interpretations of the latest Captain and Tenille or Barbara Streisand album. "Mem-o-ries, light the corners of our minds."

Forget misty, watercolor memories. Mine are in neon.

It might also have something to do with the sweet and lovely mural she painted all along the hallway wall that led to the kitchen. It was cartoonish—with children playing and a ribbon of rainbow swirling across the whole design. There were lots of big-eyed faces and smiles and bright colors. As a striking contrast, on the wall immediately next to the rainbow children, she painted a large reproduction of the Aztec calendar done in faithful detail—right down to the knives.

Maybe it was her brown polyester pants, with one pant leg shorter than the other, which she wore with the blue polyester shirt, the entire outfit splattered top to bottom with oil paint (along with her arms, hair, and shoes). This was her daily uniform and was worn for all occasions, though the colors of polyester were known to vary.

My mother had two rules when it came to clothing. Clothes were meant to cover your body and keep you warm. Or as my sister, Darleen, puts it, "Modest, but ugly." If it accomplished that, then what else could you ask for?

For the last few years, my sisters and I have made it an annual tradition to take my mom out for her birthday to help her pick out and buy her clothes. She thinks we're doing it to be nice. Really, we're doing it to avoid the indestructible polyester pants, the nursing shoes, and the rest-home blouses. The rest-home blouses will look good on her in about twenty more years, but we try to convince her that she isn't ready for them just yet. Sometimes, when she's about to try on an exceptionally homely dress, we have to gang up on her, which means that we all make simultaneous gagging sounds. An angelic choir, I'm sure.

I think the oddness may have begun long before any of my memories did. It might have all started when she was a kid and she was held back in kindergarten, or when she used to roast earthworms over a spit for her little plastic cowboys and Indians.

Which reminds me, while everybody else's mother was singing them to sleep with lullabies, my mother was singing us to sleep with "My Gal's a Corker" or "Why'd I Eat those Worms?" Yes, if you haven't heard the worm song before, trust me, it's a lovely song, particularly the part about sucking the guts out. As children, this might have been the last thing our impressionable little brains heard each night before we drifted off to dreamland. I imagine that knowing this would help explain a lot of things.

⊞ ⊞ ⊞

Music played an important part of our growing up. It's how we knew who was in the shower when we were teenagers. For example, if we could hear a high soprano-vibrato-chipmunk sounding voice belting out tunes from *The Sound of Music*, we knew it was my sister, Darleen. She also did a lovely rendition of "The Sun Will Come out Tomorrow" from *Annie*. Once, on Christmas Eve, she sat in the bath and belted out that song at the top of her lungs, only to find out that the relatives had stopped by and overheard her. They gave her a standing ovation when she finally stepped out of the bathroom.

My mom sang constantly. She pranced around the house singing "I Feel Pretty" and saying, "I'm petite like my ma-ma!" She'd seen *The Westside Story* when she was in high school and had never gotten over it. In fact, when she was a teen, she'd convinced her grandmother to buy her a fake black leather jacket, and she secretly carried a small pocketknife because she was so inspired by the musical that she'd decided she wanted to become a gang member.

Did I mention that my mom could whistle by the time she was thirteen months old? And at eleven months, she was humming "The Blue Danube?"

Musically, I'm not my mother's daughter. In fact, musically, I'm not even a part of the species homo sapiens.

Musically, I am the missing link.

I took piano lessons for four years without making it out of the Second Book. The teacher finally gave up and told my parents that they were wasting their money. If I had been a little older and financially independent, I would've sent that teacher flowers and a thank-you card.

My mother, though, has put her musical skills to good use, like the time she dressed up as Tiny Tim for a church variety show. No, no, not the *Dickens'* Tiny Tim, I mean the *ukulele* Tiny Tim. She looked just like him, except for the height thing. She sounded like him, too, which could be good or bad—I refuse to say which. And as she tiptoed through the tulips down the aisle, hoping for some audience participation, she made one elderly gentleman so nervous that he fell over backwards in his chair.

Ah, the power of music.

I probably should have been embarrassed that night, but I was too young and naïve. Instead, I decided that I wanted to be like her when I grew up.

I have since changed my mind—at least concerning the Tiny Tim episode.

🏐 🏐 🏐

My mom has a weakness for anything out of the ordinary. And where it concerns a life partner, like attracts like.

My dad won't openly acknowledge it, but he and my mom make the perfect team. He likes to think that he loves her anyway. He's in Gifted Denial. He won't admit that he's been plagued with a more subtle form of the condition.

When my mother is walking around with the glittered, bobbing, creative antennae on her head, my dad is the guy rolling his eyes and pretending as though he has to be oh so patient.

Yeah, well, he's been afflicted in a different manner. Several different manners, now that I think about it. But his main affliction is that of having too much wisdom and common sense for his own good. No, wait—his main affliction would be *thinking* that he had too much wisdom and common sense for his own good. In other words, trust him. He knows what he is doing. I'll give him this. Most of the time, this is true. But there are exceptions.

We were always so proud of him. When he and his partner tried their hand at calf roping at the local rodeo, we cheered for the whole six-and-a-half minutes it took to get the calf down. Yes, I realize that is longer than most calf ropers take by a good six minutes, but hey, the crowd loved them. They were better than the clowns.

By the way, my dad was raised on a farm, but he refused to let all of that experience get in his way.

When he was a kid, he used to practice lassoing the fence post while riding his horse. Or maybe it would be more accurate to say he would practice *not* lassoing the fence post. But he didn't give up, and finally one day, to his great delight, he managed to get that rope to land neatly around the elusive fence post. You know the old saying, "If at first you don't succeed, there is probably a good reason for it."

My dad should have harkened to this wise advice. Sure, he may have finally succeeded in tethering that wild and unruly fence post, but he forgot that the other end of the rope was tied to his saddle. And when the horse took off, my dad stayed with the saddle, the rope, and the fence post.

Success can be so fleeting.

🏵 🏵 🏵

You should never let a gifted and talented person try to outsmart a pig, because frankly, pigs rule. My dad tried. Man versus pig. Mano a snouto. All he wanted to do was to get the pig to move out to dry land so that he could shoot the pig without having to get into the muck to lift the dead carcass out. (This all makes ham and bacon sound so delicious, right?) Was that too much to ask? But the pig was feeling slightly uncooperative that day. I don't know why. Perhaps he got up on the wrong side of the pen, or perhaps he decided that a rifle was not a good sign. Whatever the case, he refused to budge when my dad stood on the bottom rail of the fence and leaned against the top two rails to push the butt of the rifle against the pig's snout. (Hunter's safety, anyone?) The pig backed up, only to move forward and back into the slop again. It was toying with my dad, teasing him. Go ahead;

lean just a little bit farther forward. A little more. Finally the top two rails gave way, and my dad landed face down in deep black tarry goo. When he got up, only his eyes were unsullied. I never did ask if he had his mouth open. I didn't want to know.

Pig, one. Dad, zero. Mom made him undress outside so she could hose him down.

Oh, and Dad, these stories are payback for all of those times when I was a teenager and you tormented me, like when you'd walk by the bathroom doorway when I was applying makeup and you'd say, "Give it up, Sis. It's hopeless." Or when we had company, which included boys my age, and you made me come downstairs to the front room so that you could say, "That's my daughter. Turn around, Karen. See? She'll be sixteen soon, and she's got all her teeth."

Okay, so he has his own peculiar brand of humor. He's very gifted with telemarketers. He never has to ask to be removed from their calling list.

However, my dad usually manages to control himself. Believe it or not, he's the practical one in the family. He is the one who matched the furniture to the drapes, because my mom may have been a wonderful artist, but she never quite caught on to the idea that burnt orange, cobalt blue, and alizarin crimson didn't look as good together in the living room as it did on canvas.

He was also the one who requested that Mom no longer use the sewing machine for the manufacture of our wearable items. He doesn't believe in hampering a person's creativity, but this was an emergency situation. It was desperate times and all that stuff. My mother, in a futile attempt to be practical, took on the task of making our clothing. There were six of us, so the clothing bill added up faster than the paychecks. Her first attempts involved bargain basement fabric she bought by the bolt. This worked out all right, because we were too young to realize that the Von Trapp children had us beat in this dress-alike fashion craze with their curtain couture, but things went downhill from there. My mom soon had a collection of fabrics—small pieces not quite big enough for a whole shirt or pair of pants—so she began piecing things together—a pink striped sleeve here, a frog-dotted sleeve there, a brown-striped front—you get the idea—and the dress was stitched together in purple thread. Clothing with interchangeable parts. A slightly less popular version of the "coat of many colors."

It was thanks to my dad that the sewing machine was banished to the deep recesses of the basement for a few years.

Unfortunately, it reared its ugly head again during my senior year in high school. This was a traumatic time in my life. There I was, almost grown up and struggling with the idea of becoming an adult. It was also the year of The Great Underwear Shortage. Most of you probably don't remember that year. It hit some families harder than others. With six kids, five of us girls, our family was almost devastated by it.

That was when my mother's creative genius flew to the rescue. She would *make* our underwear! One of the key ingredients in underwear, for those of you who aren't in the know, is fabric, so she ran down to the Fabric Warehouse and picked up an entire bolt of powder blue, double knit, bulletproof, satin tricot. On sale.

She found an old pattern without any envelope, hence no pictures of what the finished product would look like. Putting patterns back in envelopes requires time, time that could be better used on more creative and exciting tasks. You can't blame her though. Think about it. Can you see Einstein carefully folding each pattern and putting it neatly back in its proper envelope? Heck, he didn't even comb his hair!

So if Einstein believed that imagination was more important than knowledge, my mom was his kind of gal.

As she didn't know what the finished product would look like, she decided to play it safe. To make sure the underwear items were modest, she added four inches in length where the waists normally should have been. She made them all the same size so that we could share them (never mind that I was seventeen and my youngest sister was six). And just to make sure they were warm and durable, she doubled the already bulletproof fabric.

The modesty idea worked well. I became so modest when I was wearing those things that I learned to get dressed inside my P.E. locker. This is a tricky thing to do, but here's a helpful hint should you ever find yourself in a similar situation—if both locker doors on either side of you are open, they will provide more cover.

Well, we were now the proud owners of about thirty pairs of underwear, underwear that even I, the oldest and tallest, could stretch so long that I could pin the waistband over my shoulders like a swimsuit, and so bulky and warm that we wouldn't need a coat. What a deal—underwear for all seasons.

The good news is that we never complained of running out of underwear again. The other good news was that it was my last year at home, and when I left, the underwear stayed "behind." Sorry; I have a weakness for puns.

However, even after I flew the coop, my siblings endured through other embarrassing moments with Mom. There is one particular event which I happened to witness.

My mom had almost made it through to empty-nesthood. Hortense, the youngest, was a senior in high school when she decided that she needed some rhinestones to wear with her prom dress.

"Okay," my mom said, "We'll go to the mall and look for something, but remember, we're on a budget. Maybe we can find something on sale. Karen, do you want to come with us?"

Somehow, the pull of the mall overcame any sense that I should have had. Even though I had been out of the house and on my own for a good decade, I'd lived with this woman for enough years that I should have known what was ahead. I think the word "sale" must have seduced me. I admit it. I'm a bargain floozy.

We got in the car, and Hortense and I both mentioned to my mother that she might want to fix her hair. I mean, we were going to the *mall*. She said, "Okay." No big deal. She pulled a long banana clip out from between the seats (it must have been her emergency banana clip), gathered her hair up, and slapped that baby on so that her hair stuck straight up like a brush. She looked as if she were ready to clean ceilings with that hair-do, except that she's too short. And she was wearing polyester, of course, which added to the whole picture.

This was okay—not great—but we were used to it. Hortense and I would just walk a few steps behind, that was all.

But my mom was a woman with a mission.

We walked into the first jewelry store that we saw, with my mother leading the way. This was a fine jewelry store, with gold, silver, and big price tags.

I said, "Mom, I don't think we're going to find anything here. Let's go someplace else." I wanted to add "please," but I didn't want to sound desperate.

"You never know unless you ask," she said.

She marched right up to the salesgirl who had been eyeing us politely, marched past the cases of gold, silver, and rare gems, and said, "What do you have that's cheap?"

The girl was speechless.

Hortense and I dragged my mother out of there as fast as we could to spare the salesgirl and ourselves any further embarrassment.

It didn't stop there. We still needed jewelry. We hit every shop in the mall until there was just one place left. And guess what? They were having a jewelry sale! All of their rhinestones were half off. My mother rubbed her hands together. Let the bargaining begin!

Hortense and I stood back, not to watch her work, but more to maintain a distance for safety reasons.

My mother pointed to a necklace that didn't have a price tag. "How much?" she asked.

This time the salesgirl was sympathetic rather than shocked. She must have seen the look on Hortense's and my face as we retreated to a distance back away from my mom. She felt pity; I just know she did. She knew that all we wanted to do was get out of there as fast as we could.

Since she couldn't find the price, she looked at a similar necklace and gave us the price of that one. Forty dollars.

My mother's jaw dropped. (My mother is very expressive. She really does get out of speeding tickets by crying. The thing is, she's truly sorry, and her tears are sincere.)

The sales girl, bless her heart and her commissions, or lack thereof, said, "I'll tell you what. I'll give it to you for thirty dollars."

"We'll think about it," My mom said.

Then my mom saw another sign that said: "Buy One, Get One Half Off!" Her eyes gleamed, because she was really going to get a bargain now.

By the time we left the store, Hortense had earrings, a necklace, a ring, a bracelet, and a kitchen sink. My mother was just as satisfied as she would be after a big, turkey dinner. Hortense and I were humiliated beyond belief. The salesgirl was probably trying to figure out how she was going to cover the cost of her most recent sale.

In the years since that time, my mother has found more productive ways of channeling her creativity. She has become a gifted and talented specialist at the elementary school level. People say she has a unique ability for relating to these children. Go figure.

I always assumed that my mother was an innocent eccentric, that she was clueless to her differences. But several years ago, when she went to a gifted and talented conference, she attended a workshop on the characteristics of gifted and talented adults. She said that as the speaker went through each item on the list, it slowly dawned on her that the characteristics were describing her to a "T." She found out that it was normal to have a wide range of interests and a high curiosity level. In other words, it was okay to like bugs and rocks and want to know all about them even if you were just a housewife and had no reasonable excuse to do so. So what if all the other moms on the block didn't get it? She didn't have to fit in. She could laugh at jokes that no one else understood without feeling as though she owed everyone an explanation. She could ask questions that no one else seemed to think were important. She could now relax about the times that she had spent thinking that she was mentally deficient because she seemed to grasp concepts too quickly; she assumed that if she grasped them so much more quickly than most everyone else, it meant that she must have missed something.

My mother went through her entire childhood, and much of her adulthood, wondering what was wrong with her. Now, all those years of seeing the world differently suddenly made sense. She wasn't weird; she was intellectually and creatively gifted, and there were people who understood and said it was all right to be that way.

She had to go out in the hallway and have a good cry.

2: What Do You Mean, He's Reading?

I had no idea what "gifted and talented" meant. But I was soon to learn. I was hit in the face with it when my firstborn was just nine months old.

We were an ordinary family—two incredibly poor parents with one small baby. He really *was* small. He weighed less than five pounds when he was born, and he was full-term. He was a cute baby, of course. That much was obvious. The fact was objectively and repeatedly confirmed by both sets of grandparents. But other than being extraordinarily good looking, he exhibited no extraordinary gifts or abilities that were immediately obvious. (Did I mention that his head was flat on one side? And *still*, he was cute!)

That is, until one day, one ordinary day, when I came to realize that "ordinary" was a word that might apply to me, but never to my close kin, particularly this child. I was wearing a t-shirt that had words printed across the front, and when I picked Stanley up, he pointed to the "O"s on my shirt. "Oh," he said.

I thought, cool, what a coincidence. After all, he was only nine months old. Nine-month-olds might be able to support themselves on all four limbs, but they certainly don't know their alphabet. Remember, this is from a girl who didn't even know there *was* an alphabet until she was six.

But then he pointed to the "R"s on my shirt, and as he pointed to each one of them, he said, "ahw."

My son is lucky I didn't drop him. I had already dropped him twice by the time he was two weeks old, so he really was lucky to avoid it a third time. And no, that's not why he had a flat head.

How did he pick that stuff up?

Well, whenever I had housework to do, I used to sit him in front of the TV with the PBS channel on. I didn't want him to feel alone, and I thought the noise and the pictures would help keep him entertained. I mean, it had to be better than watching me wash dishes, right? And as *Sesame Street* came on three times a day, it was a sure bet that he would catch it at some point. Heck, some days I even watched it with him.

After seeing what a nine-month-old baby can pick up from watching TV, I'm sure glad he didn't spend his time in front of soap operas or talk shows! He would've learned a hundred different ways to be dysfunctional.

By the time Stanley reached his first birthday, he was able to recognize popular symbols like those used to advertise products, such as soda pop or fast-food chains. We couldn't drive down the street without him pointing to a fast-food place and begging to stop, and we couldn't drive the grocery cart down store aisles without his whining for certain brand-name food products.

By the time he was eighteen months old, he knew all of the basic shapes, numbers, and the entire alphabet. Of course, we were proud. Parents get proud at the drop of a hat. When he was born, I was proud of his blue eyes. When his eyes turned brown, I was proud of his brown eyes. But at two years of age, this child spent hours every day lying on the floor with the newspaper spread out in front of him so he could trace the letters with a pen. No kidding.

This was all his idea. Really, as proud as we were, we were not interested in pushing him. We knew people who did the flashcard thing in an effort to raise Superchild. My husband and I just didn't think that a preschooler needed that kind of

18

pressure. And to be honest, I didn't think that I wanted that kind of pressure either.

However, Stanley was hungry for information. We could've read books to him all day. Sometimes he'd read them back to us, and we were thrilled with his memorizing capabilities. We found out, at two-and-a-half, that he wasn't just memorizing; he was reading! As with everything else, we found out by accident. He was sitting on his Uncle Steve's lap, watching him write a list of simple words on a piece of paper. Steve's intention was to ask Stanley what the letters were. But instead of simply naming the letters, Stanley read each word on the paper!

Well.

We decided to read up on bright, gifted children or children who learned "out of sync" with what is expected for their age so we could learn more about what to do with him. And we learned that while we didn't want to push, it was important to work with him on his reading to make sure that he recognized phonetic sounds as well as the words that required memorization. This we did. And it took us all of three days to realize that he had it down just fine.

It was really humiliating when he had to correct us.

And he wasn't just reading the words; he understood them. He also understood things like punctuation. When he read aloud, he read with emotion and paused in all the right places. All of this seemed to come naturally for him, as he was probably mentally becoming each character in the book. He has always been an actor and is an incurable ham to this day (as opposed to a "cured" ham).

Now that Stanley could read at the age of two and some months, we decided that he was also capable of understanding the complexities of his bowel system and urinary tract, as well as a basic lesson in plumbing. So we sat him on the pot, gave him a book by Mr. Rogers, *Going to the Potty*, and said, "Okay, read." We were just his parents. We didn't know he was all that unusual.

It gave a new meaning to the idea of bathroom literature. He sat and swung his feet and read the instruction manual. I only wish the rest of my kids had been that easy.

They say most G/T (Gifted and Talented) kids have an obsession or a passion. For some, it's math. For some, it's music. With Stanley, the obsession was obvious early on. It was words, particularly words that had to do with the motion picture industry. It didn't take him long to get the reading thing figured out. Before he was three, he began reading the newspaper rather than just tracing the letters. He waited eagerly every day for the paper to show up. The first page he would turn to, even before his favorite *Garfield* cartoon on the comic page, was the movie section. He soon became a walking movie encyclopedia. He knew every film that was out, who starred in it, who produced it, what time it was playing and where, what it was rated, whether it was a tragedy, a comedy, or a drama, the critics' comments—you name it.

He is in high school now, and he still loves movies. He goes online to read scripts. He repeats scenes from movies word for word. And I do mean repeats. There are some days when I just can't take one more repetition of a scene from *Monty Python and the Holy Grail*, or from *Mystery Men*. He loves everything that has to do with the movies, and when he isn't taken with the noble aspiration of becoming a rock star, he wants to write, direct, produce, and star in movies.

Stanley is now the oldest of five, and four have turned out to be gifted. Since the youngest one is only two and hasn't distinguished himself yet in any way other than being an exceptionally good growler and wrestler, we aren't sure about him. But we're claiming the right to constant speculation as to his brilliant babbling and toddling skills.

None of the five children have exhibited their talents or gifted traits in the same ways. When I look at my youngest, Rupert, who is about the age now that Stanley was when he began reading, I think about how impossible it is for a two-year-old to read the way Stanley did. There is no way. But Stanley did it, and I have witnesses. I need them for my own sake more than for anyone else's. As difficult as it is to believe, back then, a two-year-old reading the newspaper seemed sort of normal once we got used to it.

Even though Stanley was different and his gifts were obvious early on, he set the stage for the others. I've learned since that children in a family almost consciously choose to be gifted in different things. If one has the reading thing in the bag, the next one picks something else so as not to have to compete. But it was Stanley who broke the trail for the others by helping us understand that with these kids, you have to expect the unexpected and then go with it. He taught us the idea of possibility—that you never know what influence their little brains are ripe for, and that each child has incredible potential and should not be pressured, but should be provided with opportunities to reach his or her potential in whatever area they choose.

Our daughter Magnolia is in the G/T program at school. Don't ask me how she managed this. She didn't read any sooner than any other child. Her favorite line is, "Huh? I don't get it." She could barely count to ten by the time she entered kindergarten. We tried to work with her, but she wasn't interested.

One of the most important factors involved in the education of a G/T child, or any child, is: "They gotta wanna." Because if they don't wanna, they ain't gonna.

Stanley broke the trail in a lot of other ways. The thing is, most of his broken trails are so far off the beaten path, no one else has ever found them.

Life with Junior Smarty Pants has always been interesting. Actually, "interesting" would be an understatement. Certainly never dull.

"Mom, how old are you?" he asked me one day when he was only seven.

"Why do you want to know?"

"Because," he said, "I'm filling out this application for you and I need to know your age."

"What application?"

"Oh, just an application."

I looked, and it was a plain piece of white paper with a few vital statistics written on it in incredibly sloppy handwriting. He was probably going to send it off to "Inadequate Mothers Anonymous" to see if they'd take me, but more than likely, I would have been overqualified.

"I'm twenty-six," I said.

"No, you're not. You're twenty-seven."

"Listen, kid, I know how old I am."

"You're twenty-seven. Think about it. What year is this?"

I thought about it. No, I did not use my fingers to help me count backwards. "Okay, so I'm twenty-seven."

The downside of having a bright child like this is that they want to correct you all the time, and the *really* down side is that they're usually right—though sometimes they can't prove they're right, so you use that to your advantage and claim victory based solely on age, size, and financial status.

❖ ❖ ❖

One of the first things you learn as a parent of a G/T child is never to fall for the "Why" question. It's a trick they know instinctively. You tell them to do something, they ask why, you tell them why, and then they proceed to outline fifteen logical reasons to support their opposing view.

You only dig yourself deeper into a hole by arguing with them, even though arguing with them isn't possible because they've got you and they know it. So you lose your temper and say what you should have said in the first place: "Why? Because I'm the Mom here!"

This isn't an appropriate response to a child who has a right to know and understand my motives? Well, tough beans. I'm the Mom.

❖ ❖ ❖

The Mom card is about the only one I can play without an argument. Otherwise, everything turns into a big debate over technicalities.

I'll say, "Please stop jumping on the floor."

The child will say, "I'm not jumping," and will continue to jump up and down as though on a trampoline.

Then I'll say, "I *said* quit jumping."

And the child will say, "I'm not jumping, I'm *bouncing*," proceeding to "*bounce*" until I use the correct terminology.

Another time I'll say, "Your room isn't clean. Look at all of the stuff under your bed."

The child will say, "You didn't tell me I had to clean under my bed." Thus we end up defining what's fair for me to expect when I wasn't specific enough.

Or I'll say, "Please quit arguing with each other."

Otto, my second son, will say, "I'm not arguing, *she* is. She won't believe me, and I'm right."

To which Magnolia will reply, "I'm not arguing, *he* is." And the conversation goes downhill from there.

☷ ☷ ☷

My mother used to quote Thumper, from *Bambi*: "If you can't say anything nice, don't say anything at all." When I try this line on my children, they immediately press their lips together and raise their eyebrows as if to tell me that it's fine; all of those true, awful, and well-deserved-by-their-antagonist things which are on the tips of their tongues will remain there unused. But they deny my right to exercise censorship on their facial expressions. Thumper never said anything about facial expressions.

☷ ☷ ☷

It's not all bad, living with kids who are smarter than you. One of the benefits is that, if you train them right, you'll never need a planner or a grocery list. They can be sort of like human Palm Pilots. You simply convince them that you are inept at lists and must rely on their superior mental faculties. They'll fall for this every time, mostly because—at least in my case—it's true.

On a more serious note, though, it's important as a parent to remember that bright children are still just children, and they still need lots of parental guidance. Sometimes they have the logic processes but lack the information. Sometimes they have the information but don't know what to do with it. A person might be born with intelligence, but remember that wisdom comes with experience. And parents usually have the experience.

When my younger brother, Myron, was about eight or nine, my parents took us to our first all-you-can-eat buffet. He was trying to serve himself a spoonful of Jell-O® but the slippery stuff wouldn't stay on the spoon long enough for him to get it from the buffet table to his plate on the tray. My dad whispered to him, "Use your hand."

Now, to a mature adult, this would suggest using your finger to help balance the serving of Jell-O® on the spoon.

But when you're nine, well, it just makes perfect sense to forget about the spoon, and the rest of civilization, and just scoop the Jell-O® up off of the platter with your hand. This is what I mean by wisdom being acquired from experience.

You know, I don't think we went to all that many buffets after that. One was apparently enough.

❇ ❇ ❇

Another example of having the information but not knowing what to do with it was when Stanley was five and Otto was almost three. We had some fruit trees that we'd sprayed for bugs, and we'd warned the children not to eat the fruit without washing it first because it had poison on the outside of it. I know, I should have used ladybugs instead of pesticide, but I didn't.

I happened to look out the kitchen window and saw Stanley and his friend Mark with a hose stuffed in Otto's open mouth. The hose was stuffed so far down that it looked as though it might have joined Otto's esophagus. Tears were running down his face and water shot out of his mouth in every direction. My first thought was that Stanley and Mark were trying to turn Otto into an aquarium, and as I was fully aware that the trachea was located immediately next to the esophagus and that lungs make really lousy aquariums, I ran out yelling at them to stop.

Stanley said, "But Mom, Otto ate some of the poison cherries!"

I calmed them all down, even Otto, who wasn't so worried about the hose-bloating as he was about dying from poison. After I assured them that everything was going to be fine, they ran off to play, and I went back into the house, thinking, "Wow, that five year old Stanley is so smart. I had no idea he was so up on poison intervention."

Later, I asked Stanley how he knew he should give Otto water to dilute the poison. Had he been reading a book on first aid? Or what?

He looked at me very seriously and said, "Well, I figured that if he didn't wash the cherries off before he ate them, he probably ought to wash them off after."

That's my boy.

🏮 🏮 🏮

One of the other benefits to having a bright child is that they often have a wonderful and zany sense of humor. This, however, is not always a benefit. Let me explain.

It was around midnight one night. Magnolia was two, yes, two. She was soundly asleep in her bed. I know because I checked on her on the way to my bed. Everyone was soundly asleep except for me. I crawled under my own covers and had just begun drifting into a deep sleep when I heard a blood-curdling scream from Magnolia's room. I jolted out of bed and ran in to check on her. What happened? Had an intruder crawled through her bedroom window? Had she been bitten by a giant, poisonous spider? What? No, she was fine. She lay there smiling sweetly in her bed with her covers pulled up to her chin. "Just kidding, Mommy. I was just kidding."

Thanks. Very funny indeed.

⊞ ⊞ ⊞

There was a similar incident when Stanley was just four and had been reading a children's book about stranger danger and staying safe. He must have been impressed, because he decided to try it out one day when we were in the shoe store. My husband and I were each holding one of his hands when he got the idea. He began kicking and screaming and yelling, "You're not my parents! You're not my parents!"

At that point it might have been in his best interest if somebody had believed him, because we didn't think it was nearly as funny as he thought it was.

Fortunately, nobody called the police. Maybe it was because Stanley was giggling between yells. Or maybe it was because his dad and I weren't nearly as patient with him as real kidnappers might have been.

When my nephew placed the proverbial tack on his mother's chair, she didn't think it was all that funny either. Well, actually, she did, but she wasn't about to let him know. Besides, it's difficult to laugh when one is in pain.

⊞ ⊞ ⊞

Now with Otto, my other son, regarding tact….

When Otto was eight, I informed him that we were expecting another baby. I was only two months along, but Otto just looked at me and said, "I *thought* you looked pregnant."

I'm hoping that he'll learn tact along with wisdom and experience before he gets married; though judging from my mother's rhinestone shopping experience, he may not ever learn. Perhaps I should have taken away desserts for a month or so to give him some experience with the consequences of tactlessness. He got off easy because he's my son, but if he ever says the same thing to any other woman, he might not live to tell the tale.

⊞ ⊞ ⊞

As a parent of a smart kid with no tact, how do you deal with the intelligence-experience gap and other possible gaffes? Well, first of all, you have to acknowledge that it *does* exist and that it *is* normal. It isn't fair to expect a five-year-old, no matter how bright he is, to have the wisdom of a thirty-five-year-old. Think of "experience" as wrinkle lines on the brain rather than on the face. They'll appear soon enough. Until then, enjoy the freshness.

🏳 🏳 🏳

There are occasions, though, when Stanley has displayed an uncanny knack for being wise to the ways of the world. When he was in fourth grade, he always played with the same kids and did what they wanted to do. One day, another kid asked Stanley to play with him, but Stanley said no because his usual group wanted him to play with them. Then the kid said, "Do you always do what other people tell you to do? Can't you think for yourself?"

To which Stanley replied, "Well, if I go and play with you, won't I just be doing what *you* want me to do?"

If he can just hold that thought for the next fifty or sixty years, he should be just fine.

🏳 🏳 🏳

Most of the time, a G/T child's sense of humor is delightful. A third-grade boy said to his mother when they went to Washington, DC, "Look, Arlington Cemetery—dead ahead!"

And a fourth-grade girl put a sign on her basement door that says, "DEATH TO ALL WHO ENTER WITHOUT KNOCK-ING!!!" When her mother asked her if "death" wasn't a bit harsh, the girl added a second sign beneath the first one that said in smaller letters, "OK, maybe not *death*, but please knock." The italics are hers.

A couple of years ago, when I was designing Valentine cards on the computer for my kids, I asked Stanley if he wanted to come up with something original.

27

"I've got one!" he said.

"What?" I asked. Big mistake. Actually, I loved it. It was the best card we did.

Picture a traditional pre-packaged Valentine card background—hearts in various shades of pink and red—but in the foreground, a large nose with glasses that have beady eyeballs behind them. The key feature is the large nose. Remember the nose. Got it?

Now what lovely message does the card say? "Pick ME to be your Valentine!" Ugh.

But you have to admit it *is* funny.

We should market them. They'd be a hit.

❇️ ❇️ ❇️

Often a G/T child's sense of humor will be advanced far beyond his or her age. Stanley was funny all of the way up through fifth grade, but none of his peers understood his jokes until about that time. He got along well with adults and teenagers because it was amazing to them to watch this tiny little kid with the huge sense of wit. Unfortunately, as soon as he made it into junior high, his humor regressed to the appropriate age level.

❇️ ❇️ ❇️

Almost out of high school now, Stanley gets strange whims now and then. The other day, he told me he wanted to put on a Santa suit and wander aimlessly around downtown in the middle of summer.

"Why?" I asked. "Aren't you getting enough attention around here?"

"I just think it would be cool," he said.

Then I think back to my mom dressed as Tiny Tim or dancing around the living room in her bubblegum-pink leotards. And I think I'm glad this eccentric stuff skipped a generation.

I also think I'd better hide the Santa suit.

3: School Days, School Days

At the age of four, Stanley was reading my husband's college textbooks, business textbooks even, if you can imagine anything more exciting than that. I don't think Stanley was particularly interested in what the books had to say, so much as he needed more challenge—bigger, more complicated words and ideas.

Then he turned five. Yippee, skippee. Kindergarten.

I took him to meet his teacher and have his kindergarten preview. She was very pleasant. Nice smile. Bright, colorful classroom. ABCs everywhere.

She sat down at a table with Stanley and reviewed the skills that every child his age should have. He failed the scissors test. His fine-motor skills were dismal. His large-motor skills were dismal. This kid was lucky if he could put one foot in front of the other without stopping to think about it.

Normally, I would have slumped farther and farther down in my seat as I watched him prove, ever more convincingly, that I had failed as a mother. Not this time. Just wait, I thought, just wait until you see what he can *do*.

She was about to test his verbal skills. "Repeat after me," she said to him. "Three little boys ran down the hill to find their dogs." Really, I can't remember the exact sentence, but I'm sure it was just about as deep and meaningful as that.

Stanley leaned closer to her paper and repeated the sentence perfectly.

"Very good!" she said. There was hope for this child after all.

Pshaw! That was nothing. She could have read a whole page of script, and he would have repeated it word for word.

She tried another sentence. Again, perfection. And a third, but this time Stanley actually hung his head over her paper before he repeated the sentence.

I thought, Aha! Now she'll catch on. She'll see just what a bright child he really is!

But instead of saying, "Why, this child is reading!" she slapped her hands down on the table in horror and exclaimed, "This child is *cheating*!"

I knew right then and there that we had the wrong teacher for Stanley, but I was too unsure of myself to make any waves. He was my first child, and my learning experience. He can put that on his resume someday: "I have served as a learning experience for several years, offering on-the-spot training for inflexible teachers, confused parents, and other troubled adults."

I did think about trying to skip him up a grade or two, but he was small for his age already, and I believe they expect first and second graders to be able to use scissors without inflicting pain upon themselves or upon those watching them.

Stanley didn't fail kindergarten, but he came close. He never turned in his papers, because he hated cold cereal, and his teacher gave a fruit loop to every child who successfully completed and turned in his or her assignment. He refused to color the giant beetle project anything but black. But he did sit patiently through a whole year of watching his teacher flip ABC flashcards and listening to "Aaaaah," and "Buhhh," and "Kuh."

At the first parent-teacher conference, I spoke to the teacher about his already having certain things down pat, and was there any way he could be working on something slightly more advanced?

She looked at me condescendingly. Obviously she had run into parents like me before. "No," she said. "We need to make sure he understands his letters first."

"But if he can read college textbooks without stumbling over the pronunciation of words, wouldn't that make a person think that he has his vowels and consonants figured out?"

"Rules are rules." No room for diversity here. Every peg must conform to the traditional hole. Somebody hand her a file—or a rasp!

I had another concern. "I'm worried about his handwriting. It's practically illegible. Is there anything we can do for him?"

"I wouldn't worry about that if I were you. He's in kindergarten. Most kindergartners have bad handwriting. They're just learning."

"Yes, I know," I said, "but he's been writing letters since he was almost two. He's had years of practice, and still his writing is awful."

"Well, he has plenty of time to improve. He's only in kindergarten, remember."

Okay, I get the point. My son has just turned six. He isn't expected to exceed the requirements for a six-year-old. In fact, she didn't *want* him to exceed those requirements, and any kid who got out of line and tried to run a little bit faster was going to get a good tug on his leash.

I realize that this is sounding pretty bad on the teacher side of things, but it isn't an exaggeration. Fortunately for the world and for other parents of bright kids, I believe this type of teacher is the exception rather than the rule.

I was greatly relieved when I met Stanley's first-grade teacher. No, she didn't know what to do with him either, but at least she was open for suggestions. She scheduled meetings with the school counselor, the principal, and me so that we could all discuss strategies for Stanley's education. None of them had answers, but they were willing to try new things. "What do you want us to do?" they asked. "Tell us and we'll do it."

I said, "You're looking at me?"

One of the things we did work up was a different spelling list for Stanley. Because of the teacher's limited time, I volunteered to take over part of this responsibility. Every week I hunted down the most difficult words that I could find in the dictionary. I gave Stanley the list, we reviewed them together, more for my sake than for his, and his teacher gave him a test on the words at school.

I remember trying to spit out the word "sphygmomanometer." And the only reason that I spelled it correctly just now is because I let Stanley read this and he corrected it for me. Oh, and just in case you were curious, it's the thing you measure blood pressure with. Go ahead and use it in a conversation. Impress your friends.

Stanley's teacher made a big difference for him that year. She may not have known how best to help him in his education, but she had a genuine smile rather than a professional one, and she continued smiling at him even when he didn't fit in. She even offered to let him do his work on a tape recorder, so that his handwriting wouldn't hold him back. But as much as I appreciated her offer, I was more concerned about his overcoming his handicap rather than working around it. Eventually he was going to have to deal with it. His only other option was to grow up and become a doctor.

I was tempted to go along with the tape recording, however, when I saw the papers that he brought home with handwriting on one side and very recognizable drawings of body parts on the other side. I was hoping against hope that his teacher hadn't turned his papers over. Maybe she had, and that was the *real* reason she suggested the tape-recording business.

Stanley's handwriting didn't improve. None of his physical abilities did. I remember helping out in one of his P.E. classes in second grade. It was jump rope day. All of the other kids skipped merrily away, while Stanley stared at the rope lying menacingly on the floor in front of his feet. He looked at the thing as if it were the Mississippi River at its widest point. He could almost swing the rope over his head without a problem, but as soon as it got to his feet, he froze. After summoning up every ounce of concentration, he would make an attempt to jump over it with both feet at the same time, but it didn't work. No matter how much he thought about the process of jumping, he couldn't make his legs and feet cooperate.

The really cool part was the other kids. The boys gathered around him and encouraged him and gave him advice. He still didn't make any progress, but as they say, it's the thought that counts.

Perhaps if he'd had a pair of ruby slippers he could have merely clicked his heels together three times…but wait, anything that involved heel clicking would have been hopeless.

I tried to get some special help for him from the school. They helped other kids, but they wouldn't accept Stanley into the program. He was too smart, they said. They only accepted kids whose grades were lower because of their motor skills. I said that his grades *were* lower because of his motor skills. If the teacher could read his writing, he'd *really* do well.

But it was no go. In order to get help in one area, Stanley would have to fail everywhere. To me, this was about as intelligent as saying that in order for a kid to be gifted, he had to be gifted in everything.

In third grade, Stanley got the teacher that every child should have at least once. This guy had a love of learning. He was curious. He was open to opportunities. He was different. To him, teaching wasn't a career so much as it was an education. No ruts.

He was the kind of teacher that, when a floppy disk for the computer didn't work, he would stop whatever discussion the class was having and ask them to gather around his desk so they could watch him take the floppy disk apart and see what was inside.

Then, halfway through the year, we moved. Thank goodness we moved to a school that had a G/T specialist. What a relief to finally have someone to talk to about my children, someone who knew what to do with them.

It just happened to be the same elementary school where my mother worked as a Title One aide and now works as a G/T specialist as well. The elastic that stretched across a generation finally snapped back and brought the little G/T grandchildren under the wings of the hen in the oil-paint-spattered, lopsided, polyester pants.

The strange ones were reunited.

Ten years later, Stanley's coordination is still behind that of his peers. His handwriting has improved only enough to become almost legible. Part of his problem is that his brain always runs faster than his fingers, which makes writing words down one letter at a time a tedious and mentally painful process for him.

Give him a keyboard, and he soars with his writing.

Give him a pair of running shoes, and he'll use them for paperweights. His large motor skills have made some progress with time, but I still don't think he can manage a jump rope or a balance beam. However, ask him to show you some physical humor, and his body becomes a tool in the hands of an artist.

The good news is that Stanley doesn't seem concerned about his physical progress. He is capable of doing what he enjoys, and to him, that's what really counts—though he was a little disappointed when he, Otto, and their dad had a belly dancing contest the other night. Stanley lost. His stomach was so lean that he couldn't suck it in, and there wasn't a whole lot to push out. This is going to be a real setback if he ever decides that he wants to make a career of performing the Dance of the Seven Veils. It's a sad day when we have to scratch that one off the list.

Thankfully, the SATs don't cover physical skills.

I just hope he doesn't get bored during the test and draw pictures on the back of his paper.

4: Just So I Win

Otto hit earth life just three months before Stanley's third birthday. This kid was a Ying to Stanley's Yang. He was almost twice Stanley's birth weight. I certainly hoped that was as big as any child of mine would be at birth.

As he grew, (and grew,) and developed, I anxiously watched every step of his progress for signs of brilliance. I didn't expect him to be like Stanley, so there was no pressure or anything, but I did expect a few telltale signs of intelligence—some little out-of-the-ordinary exhibitions of genius. Would an in-depth understanding of the theory of relativity by age three be too much to ask?

By four, then?

But Otto, demonstrating his characteristic perpetual stubborninity (okay, so I made that word up), refused to cooperate. With the exception of being extremely adept at stealing food off his brother's plate (Stanley didn't notice and wouldn't have cared if he had), Otto acted like a perfectly normal child. Well, almost normal. For a year or two, I thought I was raising a future inmate of the state penitentiary. It was his temper.

Wait, I'm not giving Otto enough credit. By the time he was eighteen months old, he was able to shove an entire banana into his mouth without chewing or swallowing. We were very impressed. It was some kind of talent.

This kid was anger-gifted. Actually, he was probably no angrier than any other child; he was just more determined to keep a tantrum going until he got his way. Call it *stubborn-gifted.*

I tried everything I could think of. Reasoning was no use. Time-outs didn't work. He wouldn't stay put, and his little fists and feet threatened every object and person within striking distance. Finally it came to sitting on the kid until he calmed down. Not squashing him, mind you, just a mild form of sitting which was enough to keep him on the handy-dandy time-out chair. And you have to understand that by the time he was four, he was stronger than I was. Sometimes it took an hour until he'd decide that maybe the fight wasn't worth it.

And all the while, this image of him in a black and white striped pajama outfit flitted through my mind.

Strangely enough, Otto was my sweetest child, too. He'd be full of hugs and "I love you, Mom"s in between the tantrums. I thought, "Okay, so he'll write me beautiful and repentant letters from prison."

Being temperamental wasn't enough. This child was also a confirmed introvert. If anyone he didn't know tried to talk to him, he'd hide his head or turn away. In the church nursery, he would sit in the corner with his back to the teacher. They cajoled, they coaxed, they even tried bribery. All for naught. When he finally did come out of his shell, it was only to disrupt the class. Every woman in there tried to love him into good behavior and social conformity, but they met with no success. I suggested everything I knew, but if I wasn't right there, on the spot, it was ineffective.

Finally one Sunday, one of the men caught Otto acting up. The man walked over to Otto, picked him up, and hauled him over his shoulder with Otto kicking and screaming the whole way. He placed Otto in a corner and said, "We don't act that way. When you're done, you can go back and join everyone else."

Otto was in awe. For some reason, he decided he kind of liked that guy. He finally met an adult whom he could respect.

Thankfully, Otto pulled himself together before he entered kindergarten.

Otto's stubbornness, I've found, can work both ways. First, he was determined to win with tantrums, and next, he became determined to win with self-control.

With Otto, the key is to win.

🏠 🏠 🏠

Stanley is determined to win too, as long as it doesn't require breaking a sweat.

Stanley is the better listener. I tell him to do something, or not to do something, and he mumbles, "Okay," and goes along his merry way. Does he do what I ask? Well, no, but he sure is easy to get along with. Except, perhaps when he's acting like the teenager that he is.

Otto, on the other hand, is the innocent victim, the justice-loving lawyer, the precise-definitions guy, and the I-can-keep-this-argument-going-all-day-if-I-want-to kind of kid. He loves to argue.

For example, let's say I hear a scream of pain coming from downstairs. This scream more than likely is coming from Magnolia, the innocent and easily-injured little sister. She says Otto kicked her. I say, "Otto, please don't kick your sister." Simple and direct, right? Is there any confusion there about what I meant?

But Otto replies, "I didn't kick her."

"Well, then, what did you do?"

"I just nudged her with my foot."

"Well, don't nudge her with your foot."

So then he goes into a long and detailed description of how he came to nudge her with his foot, and how, if he really nudged her at all, it was only a slight nudge and should have been painless, and of course, how any foot-nudge on his part would have been sheerly accidental, because he's not the kind of guy who would nudge his little sister with his foot without justifiable cause, unless it was through clumsiness on her part. Then he'll try to convince me that, in fact, he wasn't the one who nudged her, but it was actually *she* who bumped into *his* foot, and now that he thinks of it, his foot hurts, and shouldn't *she* get into some kind of trouble for bumping into *his* foot like that and causing him injury?

At which point, I concede defeat. (Defeet?)

I don't admit to Otto that I concede, but inside, I know that I have lost. Why? Because inside, I have almost forgotten what the problem was to begin with, and by this time it hurts my brain to sort it all out

However, as I said, the stubbornness goes both ways. Otto is also the 4.0 grade point average kid. He's the algebra whiz. He's the soccer player who, as a goalie, has been known to kick the ball all of the way across the field and to the other team's goalie box. He's the kid who doesn't think he can, but he doesn't give up easily, and then afterwards says, "I knew I could." He can't just *read* books, he has to break the school record for reading. He's the one who asks for holographic film developer for Christmas so he can get ready for the upcoming science fair. And let me tell you, it would be a whole lot easier if he'd ask for Legos® or CDs or something. You can't get holographic film developer at Wal-Mart.

Otto is also the empathetic one. During his book-reading spree, he picked up *Flowers for Algernon*, a story about a mentally-impaired man who, with the help of science, temporarily becomes incredibly intelligent. The more intelligent he becomes, the more he realizes what he was missing out on in his former life. Gradually, the intelligence wears off, and he once again becomes the man he was at the beginning of the story.

After reading that book, Otto told me that he wanted to be home schooled.

"Why?" I asked, "If you were home schooled, you'd be missing out on sports, band, and cute girls."

"I don't care. I just want to learn more and be smarter."

This was good, but it sounded a bit fishy, so I asked, "How come you want to learn so much? What is it that you want to learn?"

"I want to figure out how to make other people smart like Charlie in the book, but I want to make sure they can stay that way."

That's the sensitive, idealistic side of Otto.

▦ ▦ ▦

With the exception of his occasional teasing, Otto is my serious guy—he tries to be funny, but it just doesn't work, except every once in a while when he catches us off-guard, as opposed to Stanley's never-ending, zany sense of humor. Otto likes numbers; Stanley likes words. Otto saves his money; Stanley is a sieve with money.

I'm careful not to say these things in front of them lest the implied weak areas become self-fulfilling. In other words, I don't want one child to think that his sibling has the market cornered on a certain talent. For example, Stanley and Otto are both musically inclined, and I encourage them both to pursue it. Their personal natures still take them in different directions, even though it appears that they are both pursuing similar goals. And the fact that Stanley likes words while Otto prefers math doesn't have to imply that Otto is seriously lacking in the language arts area. It just means that they're two people with different interests.

And they look about as much alike as Moe and Curly.

Enter Larry.

Oops. I mean Magnolia. Just when I thought I'd seen both extremes, Magnolia, who is three years younger than Otto, developed her unique personality.

She was born to get Otto in trouble. When she was only eight months old, I couldn't leave her alone in a room with him. She'd already learned or figured out that if she were to scream, Otto would get blamed. We fell for the scam every time. We

39

were under the illusion that babies were sweet and innocent and dumber than fence posts. With our experience, we should have known better.

The truth came to light one evening at the dinner table, when she wasn't yet two. Magnolia sat in her highchair eating her food—though, technically, she didn't really eat her food. It was more of a process of erosion, with the runoff finding it's way to her clothing, the highchair, the floor, and all of the surrounding areas. Otto's chair was immediately next to Magnolia's highchair, and I sat across from him, so I had a pretty good view of the whole scenario. At any rate, there we all sat, enjoying another one of my delicious home-cooked meals, when Magnolia whipped her head around as though she'd just been hit, then looked at Otto and began screaming.

My husband and I glanced at each other. It was one of those "Did you see what I just saw?" looks. This little girl, at age eighteen months, was very nervy playing the game right in front of us like that. Needless to say, Otto was vindicated of all previous crimes, due to misrepresentation on the side of the prosecution.

Magnolia was also one hundred percent daddy's girl. I couldn't hug her dad when she was around without her trying to shove me away from him. If we both took her to the grocery store, she wouldn't let me near the cart. She put up with me, however, when I was the only one around. (Nowadays, things have changed quite a bit. If she wants to go shopping, I'm her only real hope, so she's nice to me.)

As a young child of two, Magnolia often talked about the life she lived before she came to live with us, the one with the Rabbit family. I don't know a whole lot about this Rabbit family except that they were obviously a million times more perfect than we were. I don't think she was telling us the whole truth, though, because at some point, Magnolia and this Rabbit family must have seen hard times, times when food was scarce. That would be the only way to explain her obsession with hoarding food when she was two. (Two was a very interesting year with Magnolia.)

One day I found a tomato, wrapped in a sandwich bag and twist-tied, hiding behind the portable dishwasher. It was accompanied by a bottle of mustard. Another day I sat down at my sewing machine (yes, I do sew, despite my traumatic experiences as a child), and placed my foot on the foot pedal, only to hear a crunch. It was a pack of graham crackers. She was even known to keep real eggs in her room, cleverly hiding them with the white plastic toy eggs that came with her toy dishes.

She never ate any of this food; she just hid it in various places around the house. Either it was for her other family, the Rabbit family, or she was making plans to run off with the circus when it came to town and was slowly building up her stash of provisions.

One time my husband caught her making off with an armful of oranges. She froze into an unblinking statue, and she remained that way, even when he walked over and picked her up to bring her back into the kitchen. She didn't twitch a muscle through any of it. It was her blend-in-with-the-woodwork, freeze-in-front-of-the-headlights technique. She must have learned this from the Rabbit family.

She was brilliant at hiding. The Christmas of her Terrible Twos was also the Christmas of the Incredible Shrinking Tree, which shrank one candy cane at a time. I knew who was responsible, but I only caught her once, and that was sheer luck on my part. I thought I heard someone in the front room, so I went in to check it out. Nope.

41

No one there. I investigated further, checking between couches and behind plants, but still, nothing.

"Odd," I thought, "I could have sworn I heard the faint crinkling of cellophane."

As I turned around to leave the room, my eye caught something out of place. It was Magnolia's lower extremities where a pile of presents should have been. The girl was wearing the tree like a lampshade.

Add "fearless" to Magnolia's chameleon capers. I couldn't take her anywhere, because she didn't particularly care whether or not I brought her home again. She was a toddler waiting for adventure. If I took her to a clothing store, she would disappear into the racks or run off into the "employees only" area. She was old enough to understand what "no" meant. She was old enough to understand threats. I would stand in the middle of the store and say something like this: "Okay, guess I'll be going home now. Too bad we're going to have to leave Magnolia here."

And somewhere in between the sweatshirts and the lingerie, Magnolia would be crouching with a big smile on her face, thinking, "Hey, this is great. I wonder if Mom will actually follow through this time."

And even when I added, "It's too bad we're going to have to leave Magnolia here. She's going to miss out on the ice cream cones," it was still no deal. She wouldn't come out until she had been hunted down, surrounded, and then dragged out kicking, screaming, and laughing wickedly all at the same time.

Usually this was more annoying than anything, but when my husband and I "lost" her once at Sears in the mall, it was a nightmare. We had every salesperson looking in every nook and cranny.

"Check inside the tents," I said. "Check inside the clothes racks!"

We finally found her sitting calmly in front of a television in the children's section. She looked innocent and harmless to the salespeople. Yep. They all thought *she* was *cute* and *we* were *irresponsible parents*. But I happen to know she wasn't in the children's section the whole time, because I'd checked there earlier and she was nowhere in sight.

I thought it best to leave that place before an employee discovered that some small person had built a hammock by tying all of the plus-sized women's bras together or some other mischievous act.

Up to now, I'd always thought that leashes on children looked rather inhumane, but when Magnolia came along, I was willing to accept a straight jacket on a rope.

No, the straight jacket was not for me, and no, the rope was not to replace the one I had reached the end of.

Then there was Stanley, who, at age seven, couldn't play hide-n-seek because the suspense was too much for him. He'd last about five seconds before he'd jump out of his hiding place, giggling and shouting, "Here I am! Over here! Look!"

Are these kids related?

Magnolia is my "go-getter" girl. If she wants something, she doesn't let anything hold her back. Otto wants his way all right, but he's not a risk taker. His stubbornness only reaches to the edge of his comfort zone. Stanley loves risks. If he could have his way, he'd be bungee jumping right now. He doesn't hesitate to go for what he wants, either, but rather than being a go-getter, he's more of a chip-away-er. He won't quit; he'll just annoy you until he wins.

🏁 🏁 🏁

I've tried to convince Stanley that patience is a virtue and that there is nothing more annoying than a fly that keeps buzzing around your head, but all he says is, "Okay, what's there to snack on? Isn't there anything besides fruit to snack on? What about toast? Are there any chips? How about cookies? All right then, can I make a cup of noodles? Please? Aw, come on, Mom. Don't you love me? I'll clean up my mess, I promise. Just one cup of noodles and I'll leave you alone."

"No?"

"Does that mean I can't have anything right now? Not even the cookies? Are you sure? What about...."

As I said, he's very focused when he wants something.

⊞ ⊞ ⊞

I read somewhere that some gifted children don't need as much sleep as other children. But gifted children need to understand that their parents *do* need as much sleep as other parents.

Magnolia did what she wanted, one way or another. She had no fear. She had cut her hair three times before the age of two, usually in the middle of the night when the rest of us party poopers were in bed. By the time she was five, she was so independent that she was ready to file to become an emancipated minor.

When she entered kindergarten, I was sure I'd be getting a call from the teacher about some problem. It turned out that Magnolia was a bit ticked off that it was only a half-day, but other than that, it was great. And her teachers said she was a gem. Go figure.

Of course, there was a little kissing incident. No big deal, really—just a harmless kiss on the cheek from a little boy in her class. I explained to her that she was much too young for that kind of thing. There would be no more kissing until she was older.

Her face lit up, and she said, "You mean like when I'm six?"

She must have figured, hey, a few more months, no problem. I can wait *that* long.

⊞ ⊞ ⊞

Speaking of her advanced problem solving and reasoning abilities, one night we were driving in the car and Magnolia was being particularly non-compliant. (Non-compliant is about the only word that works here. She didn't argue, she just ignored. Her slogan would have been "Uh huh, whatever, Mom.") So my husband tapped on the brakes just enough to slow the car, making the traditional fatherly effort to appear more threatening and serious, and he asked her, "Magnolia, why is it that you will listen to your teachers at school, but you won't listen to your mother?"

She gave the standard, "I don't know."

"Well, what do you think you should do about it?"

Then, as if she were genuinely confused about how to solve this dilemma, but also letting us know that she was willing to maintain her sense of integrity, she asked, "I should quit listening to my teachers?"

I was impressed with her answer in spite of myself.

⊞ ⊞ ⊞

Magnolia has by now reached the ripe old age of ten. If she were asked to list her hobbies, she'd say, "Amphibians, crafts, shopping, and friends. Oh, and getting Otto into trouble."

Things haven't changed much in ten years. Sibling rivalry still plays a big part in her relationship with her brother. Magnolia wants to be the virtuous Prima Donna and always be right, while Otto wants to win. It's a matter of pride on both counts, as well as a need for attention. And while nothing pleases Magnolia more than egging Otto into a fight he can't win, Otto doesn't help his case any. He may not be heavy on humor, but he *is* locked into perpetual tease mode—that is, teasing others. None of his siblings can walk by him without tripping over one of his feet or dodging his hair-tugs. He's also famous for hiding behind the front door and jumping out in front of me to scare me out of my wits, and this is not a good thing when my hands are full of groceries.

Magnolia complains about his teasing, but I don't think she minds it that much, as it gives her someone to tattle on and often works to her advantage. He makes it easy for her to appear to be the good child.

Magnolia is wise in her own way. She's the socially well-adjusted middle child. She catches on to social situations, or sibling situations, sizes them up, and then comes to amazingly accurate conclusions. However, this natural wisdom of hers is limited and is not to be confused with common sense.

⊞ ⊞ ⊞

When Magnolia asked her dad how old he was one day, he said, "Ninety-nine."

And in spite of the fact that she's a math nut and is in the fourth grade and should be old enough to know better, she said, "Oh, okay."

Then her forty-year-old dad felt guilty for misleading her and said, "Actually, Magnolia, I'm twenty-nine."

Magnolia asked me next, "Mom, how old are you?"

And I, being morally superior and proud of it, said, "I'm thirty-six."

Magnolia's reaction was, "Wow, you're sure a lot older than Dad is!"

Compare this to Stanley who, in an earlier chapter, corrected me on my age.

His hair is a titch darker than Magnolia's.

⊞ ⊞ ⊞

When one of Magnolia's friends asked her over the phone what Magnolia's sign was, Magnolia had no idea what she was talking about, so she asked, "Mom, what sign was I born under?"

"You were born under the sign of the Turkey," I said. (See? I *told* you I was morally superior to my husband.)

Magnolia, innocently and with all seriousness, relayed that information to her friend.

There was a pause. There was silence on Magnolia's end, but loud laughter projecting from the earpiece of the phone.

Magnolia gave me a look. "Mom, what sign was I *really* born under?"

Well, sometimes I get to have a little fun, too. So does my husband.

46

❖ ❖ ❖

My husband told her that the Netherlands was where Peter Pan lived. She paused for a moment, then said, "Yeah, right." She may be ditzy at times, but eventually she does catch on.

I think I've got Magnolia figured out. She'll soak in whatever information she decides is worth her time. The rest of the stuff remains unquestioned and gets filed away until she has enough patience to sort through it and toss what she doesn't need.

The inside of her brain must look similar to my desk, with thoughts scattered here and there like disheveled piles of paper. Otto's desk brain would be slightly less scattered, and there would be a whoopee cushion sitting on his office chair. And Stanley's brain space would be dominated by a huge computer monitor, because papers are much too tedious, and besides, he'd get to watch movies on the monitor.

You put the three of them together and what a mix! They could have their own show—with plenty of comedy, drama, and conflict.

There's Magnolia, who may appear to be an airhead, but who knows how to control her personal world and won't settle for anything less than what she wants. There's Stanley, the boy-genius who now wants to become a rock star. And there's Otto, the rough-and-tumble guy who now channels his energy into achieving goals and teasing, and yet is more compassionate than the average bear. Larry, Moe, and Curly? Maybe not.

Now that I think about it, the only stooges in this family are the parents.

Raisin' Brains

5: For the Love of Mummies

Pandora is my five-year-old. She prefers to be called Frances. No, that is not her middle name, it's just a name she has taken a fancy to. She is the fourth dimension that goes a step beyond my first, second, and third. Like her older sister Magnolia, Pandora is a food hoarder, but she eats it, too. I've found untold numbers of empty plastic frosting canisters under the stairs, along with an open bottle of applesauce, empty soda cans, old chocolate wrappers…the list goes on and on.

Pandora is a grump, like Otto, but she does it on purpose. It's a matter of pride. She can storm around the house carrying a chip the size of Mt. Everest on her shoulder, but if you mention that she can't have a cookie until she's happy again, she'll smile instantly, big time.

She has a memory that won't quit. Like Stanley, she has a special knack for reciting lines from movies, but instead of settling for repeating them for their own sake, she incorporates them into her daily conversation. She loves new words, phrases, and ideas.

Pandora also loves to read, or at least pretend to read. She particularly loves books about the anatomy of the human body. The other day, she said, "Mommy, we have three books on bodies—one with a few pictures of bodies, one that's all about bodies, and one that's about dead bodies."

Dead men tell no tales. But if they did, they'd have a captive audience in Pandora.

The book about dead bodies is her favorite.

I bought the graphic picture book on mummies for my older boys. I mean, when you're in sixth grade and you're studying Egypt, that stuff can be fascinating, right?

Well, yes, but when you're three years old and you love books and you find one that's full of pictures of dead and partially decayed bodies, it can be a little traumatic. It's difficult to find any books that can meet the intellectual needs of a young, eager mind and yet don't overwhelm a child with concepts beyond their experience and maturity level, especially when it comes to a subject like mummies.

When she first found the book on the shelf, Pandora brought it to me and asked me to explain what had happened to the people in the pictures. She looked a little pale, and so I said, "Oh, that's not a book you'd be interested in," and tried to slip it back onto the bookshelf and distract her with a different book. But it was not to be. I tried hiding the book in between other books and on different shelves, but she managed to find it every time. (By the way, she still calls them "mommies" rather than "mummies." I hope it isn't some kind of Freudian mistake.)

I'd walk into a room, and there she'd be, sitting on the floor with the mummy book open on her lap. "What happened to their eyeballs?" She'd ask.

"Oh, they rotted and fell out. Would you like some ice cream? A Popsicle? Maybe you could go outside and play?"

"Why did their eyeballs fall out? What did they do wrong?"

Okay, so there's no avoiding it now. I had to reassure her that these people weren't victims of a prolonged time-out.

"They didn't do anything wrong. They just died. Everyone has to die some time."

This was a new concept for Pandora. For her, people only die in the movies and are then resurrected in perfect condition for their next performance.

Thus began her fascination with death. As for me, why, I'm just thrilled to be blessed with a morbid five-year-old. Any day now I'm expecting her to refuse to wear anything that isn't black and ask to be called Morticia.

Did I mention that she happened to be born two weeks before Halloween? She was born early.

⊞ ⊞ ⊞

At first, when Pandora was getting used to the idea that she wasn't going to live forever, we did everything we could to help her adjust. The older children were very helpful. They told her that she probably wouldn't have to worry about dying until she was old like Grandma and Grandpa. Thanks, kids.

Now, a year later, she still goes up to my mother and says, out of the blue, "Grandma, I don't want you to die."

My mom, of course, is flattered and is in total agreement.

Now that Pandora is five, I think she's recovered from the initial shock. She still loves that mummy book. But just when I think she's beginning to look at it with a more clinical, less emotional point of view, she'll say something to let me know that the thought of impending death still looms heavily on her mind.

Like the other night, when I listened to her say her prayers, she said, "And please bless my whole family all to die at the same time."

I told my husband that with prayers like Pandora's, we'd better not ride in the same car together.

⊞ ⊞ ⊞

Her prayers can get pretty interesting sometimes. Recently she was in the midst of, "And please bless..." when she stopped and whispered, "Mom, what's that lady's name again?"

"What lady?" I whispered back.

"You know, the lady that comes to our house all of the time."

"What lady that comes to our house all of the time?"

"The one with hair about down to here." Pandora touched the middle of her back. By this point, we both have our eyes open.

"I'm sorry, I don't know who you mean."

"You know. The lady that comes to our house and people stand behind her."

Suddenly it dawned on me. "Oh, you mean the real estate agent?"

"Yeah, her!" Then Pandora continued in her regular prayer voice, "And please bless the real estate agent to bring lots of people to our house."

That's fine, Pandora, bless the real estate agent. Just don't ask that she be in the same car with us when we all die together as a family, because we don't have enough seat belts for one more person.

🏱 🏱 🏱

I'm under the impression that Pandora is not alone in her preoccupation with death. Other gifted children seem to find it a most fascinating subject as well.

My mother used to run an elementary G/T program in Utah. She had a wonderful zoo going. Funny, but as soon as she mentioned the idea of starting an elementary school zoo and needing contributions, hamsters and fish and lizards of all varieties were produced by all sorts of smiling, supportive parents.

This is a great fundraiser idea. Just ask people to donate unwanted pets, and then sell them to the highest bidder at an after-school auction. The kids will pressure their parents into buying the critters, and about a month later, after the parents are at their wits end because they are the ones who end up doing all of the feeding and the cleaning up of messes on the carpet, you can start the whole donation and auction process all over again. It's called Per'pet'ual School Funding. You could probably finance a whole new building that way.

🏱 🏱 🏱

Unfortunately, animals only live so long, and when you are working with a group of G/T students, the one really cool thing about dead animals is that you can take them apart to see how they work.

Now, my mom might have enjoyed frying earthworms over a spit when she was a kid, but dissecting isn't exactly on her list of all-time favorite things to do. Nonetheless, she pretended it was a wonderful learning experience for all of them, and that she "loved it to pieces." She had the kids so convinced of this that one day, when they found a long-dead horse carcass just on the outskirts of the playground, (don't ask me what it was doing there), they rounded up a posse to haul it in to my mom so she could dissect it. The playground aide, who was not so oblivious as to miss a group of children dragging a decayed horse carcass across the playground, immediately told them that under no circumstances were they to touch that thing again.

Humph! Some people have no imagination.

"But Mrs. McGillicuddy will be so happy!" the kids protested.

The playground teacher stood firm.

Little does she know, they somehow managed to disconnect the head and smuggle at least that much in to my mother's dissecting laboratory. Eventually it became an honored member of their skeleton collection.

One year, the school purchased a pet octopus. This octopus was the pride of the zoo. The kids loved the suspense of watching it stalk the fish that were placed in its tank. The thing used to wrap a tentacle around my mom's finger (probably thinking that it had hit the jackpot and had found a very largish gold-fish). They had a big contest at the school to see who could come up with the best name for the octopus. The winner was to be announced as soon as they all returned from Christmas break.

Well, somebody turned off the heat in the school during break, and the octopus experienced a little holiday hypother-mia. By the time the kids returned, it was dead in the water.

Traumatic? Nope. They put it in a bottle of alcohol and named it anyway. I guess if they shook the jar around every once in a while, they could still pretend it was alive. Personally, I think they should have stuck some goldfish in there too so he'd have food in the afterlife.

⊞ ⊞ ⊞

The kids loved it when my mom would boil down chicken bones, clean them up, and assign a project where the kids would wire them back together into a regular chicken skeleton. This is a great project, and it works much better when one of the sixth-grade teachers doesn't sneak in a few extra chicken bones from home.

Myself, I've never been one to get excited about bones and organs and all the stuff that goes with it. As a child, I wanted very badly to be a nurse, but only as long as I didn't have to deal with the blood end of things. Couldn't I just feel the patient's forehead, give them an extra blanket, and call it good? I was even willing to go so far as peeling the backs off band-aids just as long as I didn't have to look at any wounds.

I have always been a pillar of strength and fortitude.

⊞ ⊞ ⊞

Back to the delightful subject of death, when I was about four, I had a near-death experience. I picked some berries off a bush and ate them. They were blue. That's all I knew. However, later that evening, I began to worry more and more about those berries. What if they were poisonous?

Images of Snow White flitted through my mind. Hey, poison apples, poison berries—they both lead to the same conclusion.

I had heard things about poisonous berries before. Mom had said something about it at one time or another. Unfortunately, I didn't think much about poison berries until after the fact. Then, a horrible feeling of dread crept over me, and I felt a mixture of guilt, despair, and deathbed repentance.

I was sure I was going to die, and I didn't know if I should tell my parents or not. I've never been big on keeping things from people—not that I don't want to, but I just can't seem to keep my mouth shut sometimes. I finally decided that I had no option. I had to warn them so I could help them prepare for my funeral. I couldn't just outright tell them what I'd done, but maybe I could give a strong hint or two.

I found my mom sitting in the kitchen.

"Um, Mom."

"Yes, dear?"

"Um, what would happen if I, um, ate some of those berries by the driveway?" Very subtle, I know.

"What berries?"

"You know, the ones in the bushes by the driveway."

This really cleared things up for her, as our driveway was a quarter of a mile long, and the entire length was lined with wild bushes, three or four deep. I had just narrowed it down to about three hundred possible bushes, and I'm sure she appreciated the accuracy.

"Just don't eat any wild berries," she said, "without coming to me first so that I can check them out."

"Oh, sure thing, Mom, no problem," or such words as a four-year-old would say. I assured her that I would never do anything like that, and then I bravely went back to watch the TV and to die alone. I waited, and I waited. To my surprise, nothing happened. Maybe it was going to happen later that night.

So being the stoic little soldier that I was, I went to bed that night without any fuss. I kissed my mother for the last time. I brushed my teeth, I put on my pajamas, and I crawled into my bed and pulled the covers up to my chin.

My concept of death at that age was not well developed. I hadn't much experience with it, as I was still alive. And being so young, I had never discussed it with my parents. I had to leave it up to my imagination to fill me in on the details. I decided that death was something that probably only happened at night, and then an angel/cherub type person with a halo, harp, wings, and a silky blue ribbon to cover its private parts would come down to find me in my bed and carry me away.

Every night for at least a month I marched solemnly off to bed, a child martyr, knowing this was the night the angel would come. (This was especially satisfying on those nights when my mom was grouchy and I felt a little abused.) I would lie awake in my bed, all alone, knowing that I was doing the right thing by not worrying anybody. I marveled at my own courage at facing such a thing alone. I even cried a few tears of self-pity. And I waited.

Nothing happened.

As I was on the brink of extinction, I figured I could afford to be patient. I went on with my life. I ate breakfast in the morning. I ran outside and played, just like I did every other day of my life. But at night, I lay in bed and waited patiently for the angel to appear.

I finally gave it up. I must admit that by that time, I was slightly disappointed. I didn't particularly want to die, but I *was* looking forward to meeting that angel. I'd never seen one before. And as Santa and the Easter Bunny came but once a year, my opportunities to catch sight of fantastical creatures were limited.

I'm surprised that I didn't lose my faith in the tooth fairy after that experience.

Now that I'm older and more mature, death itself doesn't worry me so much. But dying scares me to pieces.

I have a list of fears that feed this. Short list: I'm afraid of heights, I'm afraid of water, and I'm afraid of being eaten by a shark. (I am *not* afraid of blueberries.)

In other words, I don't ever want to have to fly in a plane over the ocean. If I ever get to Europe it'll be because the continents have drifted back together.

I remember when I saw the movie *Jaws* on TV for the first time. I was about thirteen years old, and every time they played that awful music, I ran and hid behind the recliner.

Okay, so maybe I'm not the best person in the world to calm Pandora's fears, but I do what I can, which probably explains her amazing ability to come to terms with the whole thing.

I sat Pandora down one day and tried to explain death. I wanted her to understand our religious beliefs about what happens after we die. There would be no visions of a cupid hanging over her head at night if I could help it. I thought it might be of some comfort to her to know that our religion teaches that there is life after death, so I went over the whole process in as much detail as I could. (And considering my experience in the matter, that wasn't a lot of detail.) After I was done, I asked her, "There, does that help?"

She looked at me and nodded yes.

Relieved, I said, "Okay then, now do you understand what happens to you after you die?"

"Yes," she said, "your eyeballs fall out."

6: Hocus, Focus

When Stanley was three, it would often take him ten minutes just to get in or out of the car. It wasn't that the process was too complicated or that he didn't have the motor skills to manage; no, it was because there were so many interesting things to think about between having both feet planted firmly on the driveway and having his rear planted firmly on the back seat upholstery.

Now, at the age of sixteen, he has the same problem going up or down stairs. Nothing's changed except the locations of the distractions.

You can tell when it's happening. His footsteps begin to get slower and slower until he stops, and his face becomes slack-jawed and achieves a glazed-over look.

I have no idea what he's thinking about. I'm afraid that if I ask, he might tell me. I've made that mistake before.

Often, it's something incredibly deep, like one little girl I know who came out of a similar trance to ask her mother if Santa Claus had any children. This same girl goes into a trance often enough that her mother has named the condition "Planet Stephanie." If you ask her what she's thinking about, she'll say, "I'm organizing my planet." Or, "I'm singing in my head." (Can you see Fred Astaire now? "I'm si-i-inging in my brain, just singing in my brain! What a glorious feeling, I'm drifting again. La la la de da da….)

Stanley also has a problem walking through doorways. He himself can usually make it through the doorway just fine. The problem arises when somebody else tries walking in behind him. He'll just about hit the person in the face with the door nearly every time. Mostly, I believe (and I'm his mom, so I have to give him the benefit of the doubt), mostly it's because he just isn't aware that somebody else is there. If he does hit someone, he doesn't even know it. I've told him repeatedly that he needs to watch himself and always hold doors open, especially for women. He says, "Okay," but I have yet to see him remember. I have been the victim of this focus issue several times myself. The other day, he actually let the door shut on a close-to- elderly woman (me). Thud. He had no clue. It's too bad I wasn't using a walker of some sort. It would have helped absorb the blow.

I think it might be a good idea if people adopted a habit of shouting, "Halloo!" when they think they are walking into or out of a building behind someone who looks as if they could be intellectually or creatively gifted. Or maybe it would be better to have those distractible individuals wear blinking neon badges, the kind they give you in restaurants when you're waiting for a table, one on the front and one on the back, so people can look out for themselves.

Stanley is often somewhere way (*way, way*) out in left field. When he was eight years old and decided he wanted to try baseball, this was literally the case. He only managed to hit the ball once during the season, and when he did, everyone was so shocked, including himself, that it took a few seconds for the coach to come to his senses and shout, "Run!"

When Stanley played outfield (left field, of course), he was so far outfield that he was in the next game over. It was a matter of him running out as far as he could, stopping to stare at the clouds for an inning, maybe lying down on his back to get a better view of them, and then running back to the line-up after having his name called several times.

He tried soccer one year and was equally brilliant. He would stand in some out-of-the-way place on the soccer field with a blank but blissful expression on his face until he was yanked back into reality when the soccer ball happened to roll near. He'd hurry and kick it to get it away from him so that he'd be left alone and could go back to his thoughts.

Believe me, being a soccer mom with a son like that is an entirely different thing.

Sports were very beneficial for him. They gave him some private time to daydream, and he got a couple of really cool shirts, not to mention the pizza parties at the end of the season.

I've heard it said that one of the things that gifted kids need to learn is to focus. This isn't the real problem.

Nope.

Gifted kids need to learn to *unfocus*—at least long enough for them to get a spoon from a bowl to their mouths. Yes, unfocus, as in pulling them out of their daydream state where their high levels of concentration are pulling a covert operation. Unfortunately, the daydream state is more difficult for parents and teachers to recognize than the night dream state, as you don't have the rapid eye movements, only rapid brain movements.

Somehow, and I haven't figured this one out yet, parents and teachers have to learn how to distract these kids from their foci of choice and to redirect their attention to important life skills, like brushing that second tooth, and then the third....

You know what I'm talking about. Sometimes their brains are in fifth gear and don't slow down for corners, but their bodies are in neutral.

❖ ❖ ❖

Like one boy I know, Alfred, who was so far away when his dad tried to speak to him one night at the dinner table that his dad finally asked him, "What's the matter with you, Alfred? You got wax in your ears?"

Alfred, who must have been on a return trip to Earth at that very moment, promptly stood up and hit his sister along side the head.

"Alfred! What did you do that for?" his mom asked.

"Dad said to whack her on the ears."

Get it? (Wax in your ears?)

Kids pick the oddest moments to become obedient.

❖ ❖ ❖

Focus, particularly when combined with an intense imagination, is why gifted kids worry so much. It's why, twice a year, Stanley thinks he has cancer. He dwells on every little bump and irregularity until it has magnified itself in his brain. It's why Pandora can't let go of death. It's why my friend, Millie, was able to develop symptoms for every major, fatal disease after reading a medical reference guide. It's also why this same Millie spent days as a young child waiting for the aliens to come and take her away. She knew that there was no place to hide, because aliens weren't so stupid that they wouldn't think to look for her in her parents' bed. Why, even Sasquatch would probably think to look there.

Helpful hint: Don't let gifted children watch shows such as *Unsolved Mysteries*. And please, keep medical reference books hidden somewhere in a locked cabinet.

The focus/imagination combo can be devastating. Some kids become so focused on things that are unrealistic, yet pleasant, that they don't take time to work on the more practical side of life and thus spend their days in a dream world. Then there are others who become so focused on things that are worrisome that they either become pessimists or perfectionists and drive everyone else nuts.

My husband likes to worry about things that haven't happened yet. I really think he enjoys it. I told him that he's not a pessimist; he's an optimist in denial.

As for me, the glass may be half full, or it may be half empty. Either way, it's one more glass that has to be washed.

When I went to a meeting on perfectionism sponsored by our local G/T support group, I only went to be a part of the group—you know, to support the group. However, I discovered a little something—that my husband and I both qualify as perfectionists, though I have a more laid back form of the disease. My form of it is referred to as "intermittent perfectionism." I'm only a perfectionist when I'm willing to put the energy out.

Prior to this meeting, my spouse and I had always figured that we couldn't possibly be perfectionists because we were so flawed, blast it all. We thought we were only Perfectionist Wanna-bes. But when I brought home some test questions for my husband, he answered "yes" to every one of them without blinking

"You're a perfectionist," I said.

"No, I'm not."

"Yes, you are. You got a one hundred percent on the test."

"That's no test. Anybody else would have answered the same way. Those are all 'yes' questions."

I said, "Aha! See? You've got it so bad, you assume everyone else thinks the way you do. You don't even realize that there is another way to be."

"But all I can see is where I should be doing better."

"Precisely," I said, "You've got to start giving yourself credit for the good stuff, too."

I've decided to follow my own advice, but instead of the credit, I'll take chocolate.

🏮 🏮 🏮

Are children afflicted with occasional perfectionism?

Otto and Pandora are the two children in our family most likely to be disappointed if things don't run perfectly. Otto's desire to either be the best or not bother is a two-edged sword. As his mom, it's my job to figure out how to get the boy to put

63

effort into things that have to be done, whether or not he excels in those areas. I have to support him in his competitive efforts, yet also teach him how to be a good loser.

And Pandora's artwork is incredible for a five-year-old. It should be, because she'll draw the same pictures over and over again until she's happy with them—that is, perfect. But as long as she doesn't get stressed, discouraged, or overwhelmed by the process, I'm willing to support her in her search for perfection.

Now, where was I?

Ah, yes. Focus. Extreme concentration. Intense desire.

Focus is why my younger sister, Edna, was able to escape from my mom seventeen times in one hour. Escape here means out of the room, out of the house, and down the road. Seventeen times. My mom counted.

Hey, Edna had a goal, she was focused, and she went. Presto. Change-O. Poof. Gone.

Focus is why Edna's daughter, Wilhelmina, a three-year-old who cannot adequately be described with mere words, has a difficult time completing toilet tasks. The problem lies in the mirror on the wall facing the toilet. You guessed it. Every time Wilhelmina takes a seat, she notices the mirror and, more importantly, sees her face there. She then has to produce, study, and admire every facial expression possible for a three-year-old to make—which is close to a hundred different "looks." The boring business of potty training no doubt gets filed somewhere in the back of her brain, under "G" for "Give it up, Mom."

☒ ☒ ☒

Have you ever seen a one-year-old who has screaming fits when a commercial comes on ESPN and interrupts a professional baseball game? Heck, *I* can't sit still through one of those, not even when I have a whole pan full of fudge brownies and a half gallon of milk to help keep me occupied. (However, if someone is willing to provide the brownies and milk, I am at least willing to try.)

This same kid, son of a friend of mine, could hit a ball at eleven months old. He swings, he runs, he slides home. And if no one is around to throw him a real ball, he pretends. He swings, his mouth pops open, and his eyes follow an invisible ball as it flies up into the air and lands in the grandstands. He practices in front of the oven window so he can look at his reflection and check out his form.

Any major league scouts out there? Hey, if so, will you give me a finder's fee?

With all of this incredible ability to focus on what they're interested in, why can't we manage to direct their attention to simple daily tasks we want them to do?

It's because we say really stupid things like, "Please clean your room."

You want to know what a gifted child will hear? They'll hear, "Pleeeeease cleeee…." Just like that. Sort of like the sound of a tape in a cassette player when the batteries are going out. And they never do listen long enough to hear the end of the sentence.

So, you think, okay, I'll make sure I have eye contact. I'll speak slowly and repeat myself several times. I'll even make her repeat it back to me, so I know she understood what I said.

Very good. You've gotten through to her. Now, let's see if you can get her to remember that sentence all the way from you to her bedroom.

Some parents and teachers are convinced that these out-of-focus kids have ADD or ADHD. But really, their only attention problem is just that they don't focus on what YOU want them to focus on at a given point in time. They focus fine on what THEY want to focus on. Every time.

There are papers written by Ph.D. types about this whole topic. Really. ADHD and other Common Misdiagnoses of Gifted Children. I'm serious. Check it out.

⊞ ⊞ ⊞

Magnolia was much better at listening when she was three. When I'd ask her to do something, she'd say, "Yes, your Majesty."

I don't believe that term was used out of respect, but I could never prove it, so I had to let it go.

Now that she's ten, she's the one who struggles the most with this focusing deal, especially when chores are involved. There are some days though, when I actually succeed in getting her all of the way through her bedroom door before she loses her train of thought (the one I gave her), and goes back into her special la-la land.

The other day, I sent her to clean her room during Rupert's nap time. Her room is immediately next to his. Stupid mistake on my part. I don't know what I was thinking.

I don't know what she was thinking, either.

I mean, we'd been whispering for a good half hour. She knew he was asleep. And though it was an almost unheard of phenomenon, she also knew she had to clean her room. She'd gotten the message. It was clear in her brain. She walked through her bedroom door with good intentions, I just know she did.

But then she saw her wooden recorder sitting on her bed and floop! New focus.

The next thing I knew, I heard the lilting sounds of a fourth grader playing "Mary Had a Little Lamb."

I also heard the lilting sounds of her two-year-old little brother who was now wide awake.

Just a sec. I'm reliving the moment, and it's a good thing Magnolia is at school right now.

You know what? Sometimes I wonder if she doesn't do this kind of stuff on purpose. I know she means well. She can even be downright sweet when she wants to, with or without the focus. And since it's generally without the focus....

⊞ ⊞ ⊞

I was down in bed with a back problem one day. It was bad enough that I couldn't stand up without an intense amount of pain and a stoop like the Hunchback of Notre Dame. And since dirty laundry and dishes have a tendency to multiply faster than rabbits on fertility drugs, I was grateful (not to mention shocked), when Magnolia, sweet child that she is, kindly offered to clean the kitchen and wash some clothes for me.

I suppose that her enthusiasm for the task should have been enough to compensate for the clueless and wholesale destruction that ensued. I tried to convince myself of this the next day as I painfully made my way out of my bed and into the kitchen to survey the damage.

She swept and mopped the kitchen floor, but not necessarily in that order. Magnolia's method of floor cleaning is slightly less traditional than most. You see, she "mops" first, but her idea of mopping is that you dump some water on the floor and then soak it up with towels. (I did *not* teach her to mop this way. She picked it up by simply being oblivious to what was going on around her.) So after she mopped the floor (her way) and sogged up every bit of food or garbage, she swept, which meant that, using the broom as a paintbrush, she brushed the mushy particles and bits around the floor. A work of art. The thing is, it was not yet finished. She then proceeded to wipe the counters off. This meant taking a damp rag, whether it was clean or not was beside the point, and wiping all crumbs and debris onto the freshly mopped and swept floor.

A thing of beauty is a joy forever, but she didn't stop there. Not a chance. She unloaded the dishwasher too. Being intent on doing the task thoroughly, which gives a faulty implication of focus, she forgot to check to see if all of those dishes that she had put away were clean. They weren't.

After several unsuccessful attempts to straighten myself into an upright working position, I managed to get most of the dried food off of the floor, rewash the counters, and hunt down every last glass, cup, plate, and dirty eating utensil, so I could reload them in the dishwasher.

Then, just as I was about to collapse on the couch, an awful thought struck me. Oh, no. I remember she said she did the laundry, too.

Thankfully, she did not put the reds in with the whites. She left the whites intact and sitting in the dirty clothes hamper, where they remained in desperate need of attention. Meanwhile, we remained in desperate need of clean underwear. She had, however, washed and dried every sock in the sock box, whether it needed it or not.

She was so proud of herself for all she had accomplished. What else could I do but grin feebly from the fetal position on the couch where I had landed, finally, never to move again, and say, "Thanks, Magnolia. You're such a help. I really appreciate it."

Okay, so maybe it was more a matter of clenched teeth than a grin.

Her focus had been on pleasing me and being helpful. Unfortunately, it had not been on any of the tasks that she so fervently completed. It was as though she were running a triathlon where the only goal was to finish. Events? What events? Oh, yeah, those are the things you get out of the way so that you can make it to the finish line.

▦ ▦ ▦

Okay, so back to the original problem. Somehow you've got to make the "go clean your room" thing interesting enough that it can compete with all of the other brainwaves. So it means more than simply dumping the entire contents of a bedroom into the closet and shutting a door. This last cleaning method can be accomplished with an amazing assurance that one has really done something worthwhile. Especially when it takes three hours to get to the point of shutting the closet door.

Somehow, you have to get the kid to focus on something that is so absolutely unfocus-worthy to them that they don't think they could do it if they tried.

When you figure out how to pull that rabbit out of the hat, let me know. And if I should ever discover the answer, I'll let you know. I'll scream "Eureka! I've found it!" and it'll be the shout heard around the world. Moms everywhere will rejoice. It will become an international holiday.

Somebody pinch me.

⊞ ⊞ ⊞

I've seen the other side of focus too, the side where positive action follows being engrossed, and something positive is accomplished—well, sometimes positive.

It's amazing what a gifted kid *can* do when he puts his mind to it. It's as if he gets this image tattooed onto his brain, and he can't see around it.

Take my younger brother Myron, for instance. He's even more stubborn that Otto. You tell him that he can't do something, and he'll develop a sudden interest in proving you wrong. That's why he got an "A" in his freshman English class. It's also why he and I ate such good snacks after school before my mom got home.

She'd hide things, and though I tried my darndest, I could never find them. With six kids in the house, anything besides macaroni and cheese or soup or tuna fish sandwiches was a luxury. So when Mom brought home an economy size bag of chocolate chips—real ones and huge, too, at least an inch in diameter—well, we figured she wouldn't notice if a few of them were missing.

Please understand that I'm the girl who asked for a can of olives for my birthday, and I was excited to get them. A whole can, all to myself, unsupervised.

You have to understand something else. One of my Mom's alter egos was that of a food policeperson. She noticed every little swipe of frosting, every little nibbled edge of cookie. I believe she kept a file with our dental records in it so that she could identify teeth marks. And she had our fingerprints memorized.

But an ounce of prevention is worth a whole pound of missing chocolate, so she went to great pains to hide the really good stuff where our chocolate craving minds and fingers couldn't find it.

So the next day, when we got home from school, Myron and I figured we had a little time, but not much. I did a frantic search for the chocolate chips, but came up empty handed. I told Myron we had to give it up. She had us beat. He didn't say anything. Probably because he was engrossed in mentally unraveling the mystery before he actually did the footwork.

I said, "We're going to have to settle for cinnamon toast again."

My brother's motto is: "Anything you *can't* do, I can." He got up and went into the pantry. He was in there for only about five minutes and came back out with the bag of chocolate chips. How did he do that?

He set them on the counter for me. "They were in the barrel of wheat between the trash can linings."

I don't think he even wanted them that badly. It was more the idea that I couldn't find them and he did. So you think I should try to use this characteristic to my advantage? I should tell Magnolia that she can't clean her room, that I don't want her to clean her room, and that there will be severe consequences if she *does* clean her room?

Well, dream on. Magnolia, being her usual bubbly self, will either smile brightly and say, "Cool!" or she'll say, "Whatever, Mom." Somehow my kids have a tendency to only be gullible for other people.

There is one trick that works, though, sometimes. It's called "incentives." You dangle a real sugary carrot in front of their faces, and suddenly they acquire new talents, skills, and speed. Stanley gets to have a social life again after he finishes cleaning the bathrooms and his room. Magnolia will take candy or money or even a day with her dad at work. She can be bought with the snap of my fingers. Which makes me wonder if she really *can* focus on cleaning her room. Maybe she's just holding out for the rewards.

I'll bet she already belongs to some children's labor union, and someday when she gets tired of what I have to offer, she'll send in her lawyer to negotiate for better terms.

🏭 🏭 🏭

The more I think about it, the more I wonder if I would be better off just cleaning her room myself. I've done this before when her room was close to fire hazard status.

Wait, the memory of cleaning Magnolia's room is now coming back to haunt me, and now I remember why I refuse to clean it ever again. It's because the last time, I found too many dead animals. A fuzzy orange and brown caterpillar in an envelope was still in pretty good shape, but I only barely recognized the baby frog, the one I found behind a shelf in her closet, by its bone structure.

I just had a thought. If there is an archaeologist out there with nothing to do…. No takers? Well, Rupert is still young. He's only two. Maybe he'll develop an obsession for housework.

Hey, I can dream, can't I?

Pandora asked me the other day, "Mom, aren't you glad you have so many kids to help you clean the house?"

"Yes, dear," I said, with Magnolia's kitchen cleaning still fresh in my mind, along with a clear view of a whole new mountain of dirty laundry. I took a deep breath. Should I take the time to explain to Pandora here that having five kids in the house is not a labor-saving device?

71

No. Probably not.

⊞ ⊞ ⊞

Otto, the picked-on kid who thinks he is the only one who ever has to take out the garbage, asked me recently if I have heard of child labor laws.

I said, "Sure, but I have yet to witness any child labor firsthand."

Wait, what was the topic of this chapter again?

Oh, right, it was focus. Focus. Right.

⊞ ⊞ ⊞

Okay, so when it comes to "un-focusing" a gifted child, which is what we need to do, I have come to two conclusions:

1) It *is* possible to clean a room in two-minute intervals over a period of nine or ten days. (This also applies to homework, brushing teeth, etc.)

2) Clean rooms and life skills are probably both highly overrated.

⊞ ⊞ ⊞

To move on to another topic, forgetting goes hand-in-hand with focusing. It's sort of like a side effect of over- or under-focusing, with a little more free will involved. Sometimes children forget because they're absorbed in various mysteries of the universe. Other times they faux-forget, or "faux-r-get," which means that they only *claim* to have forgotten.

Gifted children have incredible memories—selective, yes, convenient, yes, annoying, yes, but incredible nonetheless.

On one hand (the hand with the string on the finger), my kids remember everything, and yet on the other hand, they can't seem to remember the simplest things.

⊞ ⊞ ⊞

Otto for the longest time couldn't remember that the term was "license plate," not "silence plate," and Magnolia still calls nail polish "poll nailish." If I bring this to her attention, she'll say, "Oh yeah," but I can see that the thought has left her mind even before it entered. Words aren't all that important to Magnolia. As far as she's concerned, vocabulary is limited only by one's imagination, and dictionaries are for wimps. If she can't think of a word to convey an idea, she'll make one up. When her arm falls asleep, and then gets tingly, she says her arm is "spicing."

When Otto was younger, this word-muddling business was more serious. During his first-grade year, he decided that he was going to be the Grim Reaper for Halloween. This was not a problem. However, when he went to school and told all his friends and his teacher that he was going to be the Green Raper, well, that was another story.

Some Halloween costumes just aren't appropriate for school.

⊞ ⊞ ⊞

On the basis of forgetfulness alone, I have decided that my husband and I must both be gifted. Why? Because when his checkbook is missing, it usually turns up at the register of the store where he made his last purchase. He keeps a planner religiously, because he knows that there's no way he'll remember half of what he's supposed to do without it. I, on the other hand, refuse to use a planner. I don't need one. I'm positive that I'll remember everything that I'm supposed to remember, and if not, one of the kids will surely remind me. Besides, if I had a planner, I would end up leaving it somewhere. But that wouldn't matter, because I would have forgotten to write anything in it. And that wouldn't matter either, because I would also forget to look at it to see if I *had* written anything in it.

I'm proud to say that as of yet, I have not forgotten any of my children or left them behind somewhere.

Like Otto and Magnolia, I struggle with remembering simple words. I was writing a magazine article one day when I had to call my friend. "I need a favor," I said.

"Sure."

"You know that thingy that sits in the window and uses water to cool off the air before it blows into the house? It's a primitive air conditioner, but it's called something else. It's a...?"

"A swamp cooler," she said. She's very patient with me.

"Thanks." I'd been racking my brain all day, trying to remember what that thing was called. I'd grown up with swamp coolers, and "swamp cooler" is not a complicated or overly-scientific term, so you'd think I could remember. But sometimes I can't find the word I need. I try to keep a writing notebook. When I get a great idea or think of some brilliant thought, I'm supposed to write it in my notebook so that it'll be there the next time my brain freezes up. Unfortunately, I forget how forgetful I am, and I never write things down. My notebook is empty. Still waiting for brilliant thoughts.

What I'm trying to say here is that I'm much more intelligent than I appear. It's just that it comes in bursts that have a tendency to quickly dim before anyone else can witness them.

You believe me, right?

Much of the time, my kids and I have "Mutual Forgetting Syndrome." This occurs when a parent issues an edict, doesn't write it down, and therefore can't remember it after a mere fifteen minutes, and where a child pretends to forget as well.

For example, let's say I tell Magnolia to clean her room. Whether or not she hears me is beside the point, because she responds to all parental commands with an automatic, "Okay. In a minute."

"In a minute" is Magnolia's way of lulling me into a state of false security. I hear her say, "Okay." I don't hear "In a minute." Hey, she said, "Okay." So I get back to the business of whatever it was I was doing, if I can remember what that was, because I know that whatever it was that I asked her to do is going to be done.

This has happened approximately fifteen billion times in our house, and I fall for it every time.

I also have a tendency to forget about punishments and groundings. I'll sometimes have a vague memory of telling Pandora, "No dessert tonight," but it usually surfaces just as she's licking the last crumb of cake off of her plate.

Pandora remembered the whole time and was counting on me to not come through for her. She made the mistake one day of clueing me in on the game plan. She had been grounded from Nintendo® for one week, because she had been exceptionally ornery while playing it. Then, on the very day she got her privilege back, she lost it again. That time, she wasn't content with a mere week's worth of grounding. She threw a tantrum and so lost the whole ball of wax.

In the fine tradition of parents everywhere who ground their children for life, I said, "Okay, Pandora, if this is the way you're going to act, you can't play Nintendo® any more. At all. Ever."

Immediately her tantrum stopped. She looked at me very calmly and said, "You'll forget."

Great. Now I was stuck with the "No More….Not Ever" decree, and I couldn't forget, and I couldn't give in, or I would lose what little remaining credibility I had as a Parental Authority Figure.

So I have made it a point not to forget, but I think I've found a way around it where I can give in eventually, and all without losing self-respect. I recently told her that I would lift the Nintendo® ban if she would go two weeks without demonstrating a certain behavior.

So there, the ball's back in her court.

And if there's one thing I will definitely take to my grave with me, it's the little sticky note that says Pandora isn't allowed to play Nintendo®—though I do hope they'll remove it from my forehead before the viewing.

⊞ ⊞ ⊞

"I forgot" is our family motto. I'm going to have to cross stitch it and frame it and hang it over our front door.

How does Stanley explain the zeros in his column in his teachers' grade books? Homework? Oh, yeeeaah. He forgot. Forgot he had any. Forgot it was due that day. Forgot where he put it.

A year or two ago, I went to a parent/teacher conference at Stanley's school. His teacher explained the situation like this: "I ask the students to turn in their assignments. Most students in the class calmly pull their folders out of their backpacks, locate the assignments, and turn them in. In the mean time, Stanley is frantically searching through his backpack, pulling out crumpled wads of notepaper, and unraveling them to see if they, by any chance, are the assignments that are due."

Nine times out of ten, they're not.

That's because his mind has been preoccupied with more important issues, such as whether or not a certain movie is going to be released this summer or the next.

⊞ ⊞ ⊞

I remember when I was a judge for a PTA "Reflections" essay contest. I was judging the literature category, and the winner was obvious. His essay was miles ahead of all of the other entries. It was beyond imaginative. It was sheer genius.

And it was missing its page numbers, so I begrudgingly had to disqualify it, and give the first place to a child who had written a merely above-average essay—a child who had remembered to read the rules and number her pages.

In other words, gifted kids can often remember what their mother was wearing on the day they were born, but don't expect them to remember which end of the fork goes into their mouths.

⊞ ⊞ ⊞

Stanley may not be able to remember to turn in his homework, but to this day, he remembers the time I cut his ear while I was trimming his hair. He still flinches when the scissors get close to the wounded area. The ear-cutting business happened about ten years ago, and it was only a small snip. I mean, really, the ear lost maybe an eighth of a teaspoon of blood at the most. It's not as though it had to be sewn back on.

It isn't just Stanley. All of my kids flinch when I snip around their ears. My grandkids will probably flinch when I cut their hair, if they even let me get close enough when I'm armed and dangerous.

Some memories last more than a lifetime. Somehow, when I cut Stanley's ear, I think I created a genetic imprint.

Gifted kids have a tendency to not only remember things for the long term, they also go for detail. Millie, the girl I mentioned earlier, went to the zoo with her grandpa when she was just about three. They were walking along, hand-in-hand, when she asked him, "Grandpa, what does p-a-c-h-y-d-e-r-m-s spell?"

He stopped and looked around to see where she was getting the letters. "Where did you see that?" he asked.

She said, "It was over the door back there where we saw the hippos and the elephants."

She had been thinking about it for at least three minutes before she asked him, and the sign was well out of sight by that time.

⊞ ⊞ ⊞

What does all this mean? It means that if you are a parent, your best hope is that your children will be so focused on other things that they will forget your shortcomings.

But more than likely, it means that if you have gifted kids or gifted siblings, all of your faults will be immortalized in fine detail, hopefully not in print, and hopefully, if in print, not at Barnes & Noble.

7: It's Only a Test

I have this image of a comic strip in my mind. It came to me the other day when I was in the shower. I don't know what it is about the shower, but that's my best thinking place. However, after looking at the water bill, my husband tells me we can't afford all that thinking.

Anyway, the comic strip goes like this:

> *First frame:* A doctor is standing in a hallway talking with a mother and a father. The parents have concerned looks on their faces.

> *Second frame:* The doctor says, "Your child is gifted."

> *Next frame:* There are no word bubbles, but the parents are looking at each other and their concern has changed to horror.

> *Fourth frame:* The father speaks up. He says, "I hope you won't be offended if we get a second opinion."

Some parents just don't want to know.

Then there's the flip side, where parents insist that their child is intellectually gifted simply by virtue of the fact that he's

79

their child. It's a matter of pride. When my mother taught her first G/T class, she had a little boy who didn't qualify, but his parents felt as if it would be a pock upon their son not to be labeled a genius, and they insisted that he be in the program. My mom was willing to let him try. The poor kid struggled as best he could to keep up. He knew his parents were counting on him. But he just couldn't do it.

⊞ ⊞ ⊞

No matter which side of the coin you're looking at, a kid needs to be allowed to excel, but he shouldn't be threatened with dis-inheritance if he doesn't excel in exactly the way *you* want him to excel. There's smart, and there's gifted. There's a difference. Smart kids can achieve just about anything they want to in life. They can be doctors, lawyers, anything. They'll be just fine. In many ways, smart is better than gifted.

Gifted kids think and learn differently, that's all. Sometimes they're way out there. And within the gifted group, you can have mildly gifted, moderately gifted, highly gifted and on up. You get the idea. The really high ones are *really* different in how they learn. Either way, smart or gifted, can work out just fine, but it can help a lot to know what kind of smart kid you're dealing with. They sure aren't all the same.

So how do you know when to nudge versus when to accept? It's difficult to be objective, even if you know what to look for. That's why they invented tests. Tests were discovered sometime after fire and the wheel, though there is some dispute on the actual timeline. The first test probably dates to the first flame of fire. A caveman rubbed two sticks together until they created sparks and began to blaze. Then another caveman said, "Cool. Let's touch it and see if it's hot."

When two of my sisters were in high school, they struggled with schoolwork. They just couldn't get it. Finally, a counselor gave them an ability test to see if it might give any clues or additional information to help the teachers deal with their shortcomings.

Yeah, well, turns out that their abilities were both well in the gifted range. Go figure.

This was a big disappointment for Hortense, because she'd been caught. She could no longer fake everyone out and get by without doing her homework and studying for her tests.

The test results hit my mom like a hammer. Here she'd been working with G/T kids all this time and she had failed to recognize it in her own children. It was an epiphany, just like the moment when she realized that she was gifted. An "Aha!" moment. It explained so much.

My mom was too close to her own children to see their behaviors as traits of giftedness. She saw them as an indefinable sort of "weirdness."

Although I was never tested as a child, I did have an opportunity to be tested rather recently as an adult. I'm proud to say that I passed with flying colors.

So what if it was a self-administered I.Q. test found on the Internet. That should count, right? No?

There are many ways to test for giftedness. The traditional way is to administer an I.Q. test of one kind or another or a group test of reasoning ability. However, even though I have allowed my children to be tested in this manner, I've only done so because it was the doorway into "the program."

Okay, and because I was curious.

Oh, all right, and because I hoped that they'd score themselves right off the end of the charts.

But the tests themselves are, well, somewhat inaccurate. This is the humble opinion of a mother and a nonprofessional, but I stand by it nonetheless. I do so because I have witnessed the thinking of a gifted mind versus the logic of the tests. Remember I said these kids think differently.

I took Stanley to a university to be tested when he was six. I felt it was necessary for me to get a note from a doctor, rather than just my word as a mere mother, to prove that my child had special learning needs in school.

They let me sit in with him and watch, as long as I promised to keep my mouth shut. This is difficult for me under normal circumstances, but it was extremely difficult in this case.

Let me sum up what I sat through with just one example. The tester asked Stanley if he knew who Christopher Columbus was.

Stanley said, "No."

I sat on my hands and bit my tongue.

When we got back in the car, I had a few questions for Stanley myself. "How come you told them you didn't know who Christopher Columbus was? You know that one."

"Well, sure," he said, "I know who he was, but I never actually met the guy."

Fortunately, Stanley stilled scored high enough on the test to raise some eyebrows, but we'll never know his real score, if there is a real score, because there hasn't been a test designed yet with his particular type of logic in mind.

Creative. Maybe peculiar would be a better word.

▦ ▦ ▦

Then there's Stanley's sense of humor, which overrides all other priorities. Accurate schmaccurate. Let's have fun with this thing, he says. Like the time he had his hearing tested when he was eight. He was supposed to raise his hand whenever he couldn't hear a sound. He had the doctor pretty worried, until she realized that he was messing the whole thing up on purpose.

I don't think that particular doctor should have been working with children.

▦ ▦ ▦

My sister Edna was another one whose gifted mind didn't mesh with testing. When she took the Iowa Test of Basic Skills in seventh grade, she took the artistic approach. She spent the entire time coloring in the ovals to make designs and patterns. She didn't give the questions a second thought. The next year she decided to make a half-hearted attempt to actually answer the questions. When the new test scores came back, she received a fifty dollar reward for being the most improved student.

Maybe cheaters never prosper, but slackers sometimes do.

※ ※ ※

When Otto was in second grade, he took the group ability test and didn't qualify for the gifted program. Close, but not quite. He was devastated. However, as Otto is the kid that is too stubborn to quit, he took the test again in third grade and made it.

They say chances are that if you have one gifted child, the siblings are often gifted, too, but may not show it in the same ways. It has something to do with sibling rivalry—if you're going to be smart, then I'm going to be the athletic one or the social one, because you've already got the smart label in the bag. Or sometimes parents don't recognize giftedness in another child, because they have the image and characteristics of the first child set as the ideal. They don't understand that there *is* no ideal. There are no two alike.

When it was time to test Magnolia, the blonde-like "Huh? I don't get it?" kid who could barely count to ten by the age of five, I had some serious doubts. But then I thought about the food hoarding and the Rabbit family and the midnight hair-cutting business, and I thought, "Go ahead and test that girl!"

She qualified. Even though she was handicapped by growing up in a home where an outlet is known as a "plug-in" (she missed that one in the vocabulary part of the test). She still made it.

And so, with all my hands-on experience with gifted children, I have developed my own test criteria, which I believe are as accurate in identifying the gifted and talented as any verbal- and mathematical-based I.Q. test questions will ever be. They blow the Renzulli/Hartman Scale right out of the water as well.

Ready for some of the sample items?

Are you sure?

Okay. Brace yourself and…go! (You will not be timed.)

🃏 If your two-year-old tries to make Jell-O® on her carpet, and she uses a large box of Berry Blue and dumps copious amounts of water over it, because everyone knows that's how one makes Jell-O® and she does all of this before you are even out of bed in the morning, she's probably gifted.

🃏 If your seven-year-old tries to help clean the Jell-O® mess up by vacuuming it with a traditional vacuum cleaner until blue gel oozes from every crevice and your house smells like raspberries-in-a-box, she's probably gifted, too.

🃏 If your eleven-year-old loves to make model cars, and he loads them with painstaking detail right down to fake fur upholstery on the bucket seats, and he goes to all of that trouble so that he can blow them up and display their melted and mangled car bodies neatly in a row on a shelf in his room, he could be either gifted or sick.

🃏 If your first-grade son gets really excited about bringing a used fabric softener sheet for show-and-tell and then gets even more excited about bringing a rubber band the next week, well, he either has a very dull life or he's gifted.

🃏 If every other five-year-old girl on the block wants a battery-operated, walking, talking, singing, dancing Whizmo the Gizmo doll for Christmas, but your five-year-old daughter just wants her very own ream of plain white paper, she's probably gifted—and you are getting off cheap.

⊞ If your four-year-old son has Social Services on speed-dial so that he can contact them every time he gets angry and decides he'd rather take his chances with foster parents, he's probably gifted.

⊞ If, by the age of three, your son has managed to start the car by himself, fill the gas tank with water, stuff the cassette player with spaghetti, accidentally set a plastic trashcan on fire (trying to burn the garbage), shampoo the couches, flush a dress down the toilet, and melt a Tonka® truck by pouring concentrated flavoring extracts into the back of it, well then, he's probably gifted. And you have my sympathies.

I'd like to thank a cousin who was the model for the last example above. Credit should be given where credit is due.

Now for some adult gifted criteria:

⊞ If your husband, an absent-minded professor type, pours sesame oil rather than maple syrup on his pancakes, and then proceeds to eat without a clue that anything is amiss, even after you tell him that there is an awfully strange smell coming from the direction of his plate, he's probably at least a little gifted.

⊞ If your mother disciplined you as a teenager by threatening to chase you down, pull your shoe off, and bite your stinky big toe, and followed through with that threat, she is probably gifted (as well as a little warped).

⊞ If the new Gifted and Talented Specialist locks herself in her office on her first day at work, and can't figure out how to unlock the door or how to dial out on her phone to call for help, she's probably not only gifted, she's perfect for the job.

▦ If your uncle mows the lawn with a helium balloon tied to the bridge of his glasses so that they won't put so much pressure on his nose, he's probably gifted.

Note: All of these examples are taken from people I actually know. Scary, huh?

▦ ▦ ▦

To show that tests are not always used or interpreted appropriately, I'll use my mom as an example. When my mother was in high school, they gave her an aptitude test to see what courses she should take. It turned out that she was mechanical engineering material in every way but one—she was a girl.

Her counselor told her that it was too bad she was girl, because that pretty much eliminated her from taking any high school classes in mechanics or engineering. Her only other options, according to this test, were to become either an artist or a mother.

It turns out she did both. Art and motherhood. Motherhood *is* an art. But what she *really* wanted to study in school was science. They said, "Sorry, but science isn't your thing. You scored poorly on that section of the aptitude test. You may take the bonehead (yes, they really did call it bonehead) science course if you want, but that's as far as you can go."

So she took bonehead science and worked her heart out. Still, they wouldn't let her take anything beyond. She's been a closet scientist ever since.

Do you know what it's like to grow up with a closet scientist as your main caregiver? As a budding ichthyologist, she claimed that she took her dead baby guppies and put them in my tuna sandwich. (Did I mention that she was also a budding stand-up comedian?) She also kept a bucket of brine fish in the refrigerator. You have no idea how smelly that can be. It is, however, a terrific diet plan. You don't even want to *think* about opening that refrigerator door unless all of the windows are open and a steady breeze is blowing. Even then, you have to be careful to make sure you aren't standing downwind.

Anyway, as a budding ornithologist, she used to clean freshly butchered chickens in one sink, while she made me peel potatoes in the other sink. Then she'd slowly stretch out and squeeze the poor bird's blood vessels and watch the stuff come out. She'd say, "Look, Karen, isn't that interesting?" (And she *says* she doesn't like to dissect.) Do you blame me when I tell you I can't eat any chicken that has telltale veins in it? I don't want to be reminded that it was once alive. And after the guppy episode, I can't eat tuna fish either. It's a wonder I can eat anything at all.

I mentioned the pea bread earlier, didn't I? How about the combination popcorn and grilled cheese sandwiches? The tuna and jellybean sandwiches? Yes, tuna and jellybean. She told us there was a surprise inside.

When she wasn't experimenting with food, she was experimenting on us. My mom couldn't resist chemicals, even if they were just the kind used for perming hair. She did a cross-test thing on all of us girls about once every two or three years. She would take one bottle of perm solution and perm just *portions* of each of our manes. Unfortunately, perm kits weren't made to be used by five people. We ended up looking like we'd all five been caught in the same lightning storm but had been hit in different spots. Either that or someone had been experimenting with electro-phrenology.

I'm just glad she didn't decide to study medicine. There might have been some serious, long term results.

I struggled with allowing Otto to take the test the second time. I went through all of those feelings that parents go through. We don't want to set a kid up for a perceived failure; we don't want to apply pressure; we don't want to make the gifted label out to be the be-all and end-all of personal worth.

And certainly, I didn't want Otto to feel like he was some sub-human species or genetically defective offspring if he didn't do everything as well as Stanley. So I told him that I knew he was pretty cool just the way he was, and if he wanted to take the test again, it was totally up to him. And since Otto isn't the kind of kid to give up, even when you really want him to give up, he decided that he was going to take the test as many times as they'd let him, until he scored well enough to get into the gifted program. He qualified on the second try.

⊞ ⊞ ⊞

There was some concern when I gave my permission to have Magnolia tested for the program. Just a few comments here and there from people who don't think every child should necessarily be tested, because it could damage a person's self-esteem if the child doesn't quite hit the high marks. This is a legitimate concern, and I can see their point. But I figure, hey, she's going to grow up and get dumped by boyfriends, she's not going to get every scholarship or job that she applies for, she may not make first string on the girls' basketball team, and she might even grow up some day to try on a size eight dress only to find that size doesn't fit anymore.

Certainly if she ends up being a writer, like me, she's going to get rejected on a regular basis by people who have no interest whatsoever in her self-esteem. (I *know* about these things. And

I've survived.) In fact, over the years I've decided that *failure* is a healthy prerequisite for anyone who wants to major in success.

The other day, I peeled a sticker off of the inside of a food container lid. It said, "Sorry, you are a non-winner. Please try again." There was something about that that irked me. I mean, sure, I felt bad that I hadn't won the million-dollar shopping spree or the new luxury sedan, but what was worse was that I felt insulted, as though the company didn't think I could handle the term "lose." Losing is a temporary thing that needs to be dealt with on occasion. It isn't something that has to be smoothed over or hidden or avoided. And keep in mind, this is coming from a person whose entire lifetime's winnings consist of a single orange whistle I won as a door prize a few years back. Okay, okay, and an occasional mini-candy bar, when I play bingo with my family. Oh, all right, and every once in a while I'll take first place at a bridal shower game. And oops, I almost forgot that order of fries that I won when I received the magic playing piece from a fast-food restaurant.

Gee, now that I think of it, I'm more of a success than I thought. I'm feeling pretty good about myself. However, I'd better not think too hard, or I might start remembering all of the times when I was a non-winner.

That's life. I've adjusted. I figure that Magnolia might as well get used to it too. Her only other option is to stick to the easy and obvious things that are pleasant and unchallenging. In fact, she could go through her entire educational career coasting through school and avoiding challenges, at least until she gets to college. Which brings us to the problem of schools being too easy for some bright kids. When things are too easy, it seems to me, it can result in laziness or other serious wastes of brain cells. If bright kids coast through school and never learn to study or never have to buckle down and think, they won't have those study and organizational skills later when they may need it them.

Like when they hit algebra or geometry or calculus for the first time. How will they know this is a subject where you *do* in fact have to spend a few hours figuring it out or working your brain? If they've never met a challenge before, they may just say, "This is too hard. I can't get an easy 'A,' so I guess I'd better drop the class."

🔠 🔠 🔠

Do I support testing for giftedness? Yes. Not only will it help you to know what sort of gifted child you have and what areas he or she is strong in, it will also show you the areas where he or she may need extra help. That information is critical to both the parents and the teachers who are working with the child, and it will help them design an educational plan.

Let's go back to those resourceful cavemen. (Meanwhile, back at the Stone Age....) There they are, gathered around this lovely, warm, new light and heat source, and one of them is sitting on a rock, sucking on his burnt finger. He's what we call the "test administrator." He now knows that the fire is hot. He has proof. Does he know exactly how hot it is? Is he able to measure it in Celsius? Nope, but he knows it's hot.

The I.Q. and ability tests operate on the same principle. You won't get an absolutely accurate reading, but you'll be able to recognize definite areas of strength and weakness, and you'll know there are some things happening in that child's brain that are well above average thinking temperature.

8: Can You Repeat the Question?

sometimes wonder what would have happened if my mom had been encouraged to pursue her dream of becoming a scientist. She might have discovered some amazing cure for the common cold. She might have developed new theories regarding the evolution of human life. She might have been the first woman to genetically engineer a cow that could produce fat-free milk.

And instead of focusing on being a mom, she might have limited herself to one child rather than six. (Hey, engineering a fat-free milk cow takes time and energy.) Being the oldest child in the family, I often pondered this in my youth and thought that being an only child might not have been too bad a deal.

However, my mom *didn't* become a scientist, I *do* have five younger siblings, and still, things have turned out pretty peachy all the way around. I get more birthday presents. And my mom has a satisfying job working with kids who need her empathy and advocacy.

In other words, my mom turned out okay (I didn't say "normal," I said "*okay*") even if she wasn't encouraged to pursue her dreams.

Still, there's something inside of me that yearns for more and better opportunities for my own kids at school, and this includes a gifted/talented program that recognizes their capabilities, learning styles, and interests and keeps things challenging.

Are my kids more gifted and talented than the most gifted kids? Well, *I* happen to think so, but in reality, probably not. They do learn things really quickly and remember them. They do get really frustrated with classwork that is too slow. And they do seem to be pretty creative in their ideas. But this gifted thing doesn't mean that they are better than other kids. Nope. They learn differently than some other kids, that's all. Some kids learn slowly, some learn quickly, some are in between. And some kids have learning disabilities in some areas and are gifted in others. There are all sorts of gifted kids, just like there are all sorts of kids, period. Some people think that people who are gifted are genius level in everything. Not true. Look at Stanley. He doesn't excel in math or athletics. But he sure is good at what he loves—which would be words, language, and music.

The point is that *all* kids should be able to learn material that's right for them and at the pace that's right for them.

I know to some people this might sound like *Brave New World Revisited* or H.G. Wells' *Time Machine*, where you have a distinction of classes of humanity, or you have the results from having distinctions. You sometimes hear these people say, "All children are gifted."

Here's what I think. I believe that everyone has gifts or exceptional personality traits of one kind or another. I believe that all children should be given special care and attention. But at least in the educational sense, all children are not "intellectually gifted" any more than all children are "learning disabled." It's a matter of semantics, I suppose.

Just as it's not fair to expect children with learning disabilities to learn the same way and at the same rate as others, it's unfair to expect gifted children to do ten extra problems (just to keep busy), especially if they already know how to do this particular kind of problem in their sleep and don't need more "practice" with it.

People who give children the label of "gifted" often receive the label of "elitist" by other people who abhor the use of labels and want everyone to be the same. For the people who don't like labels, it's sort of like saying, "Don't call people names, you name-caller, you!" But what else shall we call the G/T kids?

The children that my mom taught in Utah were called the Nerd Herd by the rest of the children. Now *that* name might satisfy *everyone*, with the possible exception of the so-called Nerd Herd.

Look at it this way: people who are good at music are called musicians, people who are good at art are called artists, and people who are good at athletics are called athletes. This leaves kids who happen to be good at thinking with the possible terms "thinkicians," "thinkists," or, uh, possibly "thinketes?" Would that be better?

Listen, if anyone is worried about people making the gifted and talented out to be a class of superior human beings, it's because they haven't spent time watching Stanley play basketball. He does what he refers to as psychological fouls. Believe me, you don't want to know. Rest assured, it's enough to stop the game as everyone looks at him and tries to figure out if he needs immediate medical attention or if he's just really weird.

"Gifted and Talented" is merely the term being used these days because no one has come up with a better one that would be widely recognized as meaning the same thing—though Nerd Herd does come in a close second.

If you think some parents get a little too proud about it, just think of them as football fans with a quarterback for a son. It's completely understandable.

It's also completely understandable if you prefer not to sit next to them during the game.

Gifted kids require different approaches to learning in the classroom. We're talking about *creative* problem solvers. They *are* good at thinking, but that doesn't mean they do well or comprehend every subject the way that it's traditionally taught. They have to hone their skills like anyone else.

For example, my younger sister Hortense was failing U.S. History in high school. Yep, she's blonde, but she's also gifted. As I mentioned, gifted kids sometimes have weak spots or even learning disabilities. It's as if their brain is way ahead in some areas but has a wiring glitch in others. Somehow, Hortense wasn't able to translate the teacher's lectures into notes on her paper, and this left her with nothing to study. She had a disability in written language. But she could draw. So a wise counselor person stepped in and taught her how to take notes in pictures rather than in words. It worked. Nobody else but Hortense and a few extremely adept cavemen or ancient Egyptians could decipher her picture notes, but that was beside the point. Her grades went up.

Stanley has always struggled with his small and large motor skills. Please don't ask him to write a legible sentence. Yet if you give him a musical instrument, his ten clumsy thumbs turn into fingers that play the notes beautifully. It's magic. Hey, manual dexterity happens.

Speaking of motor skills, I am a writer who can't type properly. I've tried. I'm still stuck with the title, "The Fastest Four Fingers in the West." I call my method "divergent typing."

My husband was razzing me the other day about my typing, so I challenged him to a race. He typed in the conventional manner, while I did my own freestyle method. We each had five minutes to type as much as we possibly could from a particular piece of material. Points were deducted for typos. Ha! I won.

Excuse me for a moment. I'm doing a mental touchdown dance.

🏱 🏱 🏱

Manual dexterity may happen, but mental dexterity is something else. Here's an example with Magnolia.

When I was studying geography with Magnolia the other day, it went something like this.

"Okay," I said, "what is a body of water surrounded on all sides by land called?" (For those of you who may be geography impaired, the answer is "lake." I'd hate to leave you in suspense.)

Magnolia leaned back in her chair and looked up at the ceiling. She was thinking. Then she said, "Can you repeat the question?"

I thought, great, she is going to be tested on this tomorrow, and this is the easiest term out of sixty she needs to learn. But very patiently (please do not ask Magnolia to verify this for you), I repeated the question.

She wrinkled up her nose and took a guess. "A valley?"

Beep! Wrong. I said, "Listen very carefully. A body of *water* that is surrounded on all sides by land."

"An island?"

"No. Here's a hint. A body of water. Got that? It's a body of water. And it happens to be surrounded by land."

She looked at me as puzzled as ever.

I said, "Lake. It's called a lake. Better write that one down."

Now Magnolia happens to be a whiz at math, which I wasn't, but she appears to be totally geography challenged, which I also wasn't. I may be now, but at one time I wasn't. Please, don't test me.

When I look into Magnolia's confused eyes, I see a brain that only hears nouns. She hears "water," and she hears "land." If she really pushes the envelope, she might hear a verb like "surrounded." However, even if all of these words register in her brain, they do so in no particular order. Water surrounded by land. Land surrounded by water. It's all the same to her. Somehow, I've got to figure out a way to help her grasp concepts that are meaningless to her.

Maybe I should try the electric shock method.

Some days I feel as if Magnolia is the pilot of a small plane, and I am the guy standing on the runway trying to flag her down with a light in each of my hands. "Over here! Hey, you, look, come over heeeeeere!" Then I dive to the ground so she won't plow me over, but just before I hit the ground, I catch a glimpse of her face and her eyes. And I realize that the eyes aren't registering anything that's in front of them, only what's behind them and inside her head. Next thing I know, the plane is back up at twenty thousand feet, and all I can do is hope that she'll have to come down for fuel eventually.

Recently, Magnolia mentioned that, for the first time in her elementary career, she was having test anxiety. She said her teacher was going too fast on the questions. When I spoke to her teacher about it, the teacher said, "That doesn't sound quite right. I give the kids plenty of time to answer questions. I think the problem is that I give a question, and Magnolia sits there and daydreams until I give the next question, and then she panics because she suddenly gets yanked back to earth and realizes that she hasn't written down any answers yet."

Yes, that would be Magnolia all right.

Fortunately, she has pulled herself together a bit since then. She's figured out that nobody's going to float her anymore. She's in fourth grade—the big league. It's either sink or dog paddle.

I remember my own fourth-grade year. I was supposed to make a puppet to represent Abraham Lincoln and use it to do a presentation for the class. I had never had an assignment like that before, but I did my best. I took a toilet paper tube and made a papier mache head with a big nose. I then painted it with watercolors and gave it the name of Lincoln. I was very proud of it. However, when I went back to school the next day and saw the elaborate, neatly done projects that the rest of the class had brought, I looked down at my mess of a puppet, newsprint still showing through the paint, no stove pipe hat or three piece suit, and hardly any recognizable features except for the nose, and I was humiliated.

It got worse when it came time to give my presentation. I bit my lip, stood up in front of the class, held my puppet sort of up where perhaps it could be seen by the people in the front row, and said, "This is my puppet, Abraham Lincoln."

That was it. Hey, I presented it, didn't I? The teacher never said what kind of presentation or how long or what it should entail, right? His exact words were, and I quote, "Do a presentation for the class."

I failed that project.

When Otto did his holography project for the science fair in seventh grade, he and I were both impressed with the results. He'd bought the chemicals, the curved lenses, the mirrors, the beam splitter, and the film. He'd set everything up, experimented, failed, experimented again, failed, until the fourth try which produced a pretty good holograph. It required an elaborate and precise setup and he had to use his talent for math and angles to figure it all out.

So how did he do at the science fair? Only so-so. We thought he had it in the bag, but once again, it was the story of the Lincoln puppet, though with a much nicer puppet. Otto got to the science fair and saw the elaborate presentations the other kids had put together. They had beautiful backdrops, catchy slogans, and neatly-typed five- or six-page reports.

He didn't know until he got there what the competition was going to be.

However, he was way ahead of Stanley, who, at the same age, hastily slopped together a science project and pasted it on a bent piece of poster board rather than the professional looking science fair board that all of the other kids used.

Stanley later described it as a shack sitting in the middle of Bel Aire.

🀫 🀫 🀫

Creative thinkers need creative instruction. When my mom was asked to help teach a section on the digestive system to a class of third graders, she placed the students right where the action was. She pushed the desks up against each other, taped garbage bags together to make a waterproof passage—a sort of fake alimentary canal—gave each kid a name badge, and then lined them up according to the names on their badges.

The kid with the badge that said "Lips" on it stood at the head of the line and was the first to get his hands on a peanut butter sandwich. His job was to pass it into the mouth area to the girls who had the Teeth and Tongue badges. The Teeth girl chopped at the food with her hands while the Tongue girl kept the food where it needed to be. Then the Salivary Glands boy squirted water into the mess to make it messier. The Throat children helped to work the food down to the Stomach, where green lemon juice was added, and when the gunk hit the Duodenum, the Liver squirted dish detergent bile into the mutilated pulp.

So it went, all the way down to the shy, quiet little girl who wore the Rectum name badge. Her job was to squeeze the final waste product into the garbage can.

She did her job with pride.

You can bet that those kids, all of them, intellectually or otherwise gifted, had a pretty in-depth understanding of what happens to any unfortunate peanut butter sandwich that happens to get caught by a pair of lips.

Because, and this is the really cool thing, when you introduce more creative instruction into a classroom, the intellectually gifted kids aren't the only ones who benefit. The intellectually or creatively gifted kids who haven't been identified, of course, also benefit. The kids who have skills and talents in other areas, in or out of the classroom, benefit. (By the way, just in case you were wondering, this would mean all of the kids.)

And the janitor benefits, because he's the guy who gets to clean up after the experiments. Job security.

▦ ▦ ▦

Clustering gifted kids in the same classroom is often a productive way to kill several birds with one stone. We could expand on the bird clichés. Birds of a feather are better flocked together. Six birds in the hand are worth twelve disbursed indiscriminately through the bushes. It's hard to fly with the turkeys when you're stuck with the eagles.

What, you don't recognize those?

One good reason to cluster gifted kids in one classroom is so that you can keep a sharp eye on all of them at the same time. One trained gifted warden is all it takes. Okay, and maybe a couple of volunteer deputies.

But it's truly helpful for these sometimes strange and unique kids to be around each other. It's the *Anne of Green Gables* kindred spirit thing. It's the *Close Encounters* thing too—it's a relief to know that you are not alone.

And sometimes the competitive spirit is helpful. A track star is going to run faster if he can feel someone else on his heels.

Then there are kids like Otto who figure, hey, if I can't be the best, why bother? Why waste my energy? Otto didn't always do well in clustering. It's that individual attention thing. In Otto's case, if the early bird gets the worm, he'd better not have to share it, because if he has to share, why, he might as well just sleep in and forget about it and let the other guy do the work.

Enhancement is another option for the gifted child. For some teachers, enhancement—sometimes called enrichment—means that a teacher gives a kid a desk in the hallway and gives him an encyclopedia to read. This, however, accomplishes little more than alienating the student from the rest of her peers and makes her feel like a behavior problem. Plus, when you put kids in a situation like that, it's as though you've put them on a treadmill and told them to run, only it doesn't matter how fast they go, because they'll never get anywhere. There's not much motivation in this type of enhancement.

They need a reason to run and a goal to reach. This is not accomplished by worksheets or busy work. Enhancement goes beyond the regular stuff and sometimes beyond the classroom, and it doesn't limit itself to the gifted kids. They just happen to be the ones who need it the most.

Okay, so what is enhancement? It's when the lesson material is broadened and deepened in an interesting way. I know teachers cringe when you tell them there is one more thing to add to their already hectic schedules, but enhancement is such an efficient teaching tool, it doesn't necessarily require more of the teacher's time.

However, it does require coloring outside of the lines and stretching the creative muscles a bit. Take the previous lesson on digestion. The kids had a chance to get into their subject a little more, to be involved, and to feel what it's like to do the work of a stomach. It suddenly became interesting for them—certainly more interesting than just learning about it from a book. Once they had done the hands-on stuff and were pretty excited, that would have been a good time to throw in some extra material on the digestive system, something starving brains could sink their teeth into, because they now had an appetite for it and could put the information into context. Each kid could pick up whatever extra information he or she chose to brain file.

The digestive example got several parts of the kids' brains going. Their sensory brain got turned on as their hands touched and moved the food along, their thinking brains kicked in as they kept the food going in order from the lips to the mouth to the throat and so on, and finally, their social/emotional brain kicked in as they interacted with the other kids in the line. The best learning involves all parts of the brain. It's a good bet that these kids will remember this digestive lesson lots longer than kids who only read about it in a book.

❖ ❖ ❖

When a student is encouraged to move ahead in the curriculum, it's called acceleration. It's another way to help gifted kids make academic progress. It's like allowing a brain to learn on fast forward instead of on pause. They get to speed walk through the stuff they already know so that they can get to the high hurdles or the pole vaulting where the challenges await them. They get to learn at their own pace—no brain-starving.

One of the ways of allowing children to accelerate their education is to "compact." Compacting is when a student is allowed to take a pre-test in a subject such as math or spelling to see if she already knows the material. If her score is high enough on the pre-test, she is then allowed to move on to something in a subject area that is more interesting to her. If she scores well on most of the test but obviously has a problem with one or two particular areas, then she can join the rest of the class when those areas are discussed.

Sometimes kids need more than compacting. Sometimes they need to be allowed to skip a whole grade level so that they can receive adequate challenges.

One of the problems of having gifted children in a regular classroom is that it can be a struggle to meet the needs of both the gifted students and the rest of the class, even when you try the creative approach. In an effort to maintain some sanity and some sense of order, teachers sometimes hold the gifted children back and tell them to wait for the rest of the class to catch up.

In other words, success is not defined by achieving or progressing; it's defined as remaining docile under duress. In this model, the gifted child is expected to sit quietly and follow along in his reader that goes on and on in one- or two-syllable words about Orville and Wilbur Wright, when really, what the kid is dying to do is build his own airplane. He already knows about Orville and Wilbur Wright. He learned about the Wrights while reading the encyclopedia the other day, back when he was in kindergarten. Now he's sitting in class as patiently as his itchy brain will let him, daydreaming about what the perfect name for his airplane would be and how he'd be flying it in battle and what color stripes would line the sides. And his teacher calls on him to read, but now he doesn't know which paragraph, because even though he fully intended to follow along, his brain has run off without his permission and taken him to another dimension in time and space.

My nephew, Percival, is like that. He's a quiet, shy boy who speaks in whispers and doesn't like to call attention to himself—unless he's at home. At home, he's Superman. And at school, in his head, he's Superman. But outwardly to others at school or around people he doesn't know, he's a quieter, meeker version of Clark Kent—minus the glasses. Still, in first grade, when the class recites the alphabet, it is more than Percival can take. It frustrates him to go so slowly. He forfeits all his reserve and rattles off the alphabet as loudly and quickly as he possibly can.

This, of course, throws all of the other kids off and disrupts the class. It also shocks the teacher, who kindly asks him to please slow down and quiet down and stay with the class.

Clark Kent, step away from the phone booth.

Fortunately, he is in a classroom with a teacher who understands gifted kids.

⊞ ⊞ ⊞

It's probably helpful when a teacher of the gifted is gifted herself. My sister, Gertrude, Percival's mom, says she knows that his teacher is gifted because, among other telltale signs, when she went to parent/teacher conference, the teacher had several bags of dirt on her desk and was *excited* about it. Gertrude thinks that I should write another book titled *Gifted Teachers: Amazing Creatures*. It could cover teachers like the local chemistry/calculus/physics teacher who has been known to drag a hockey puck on a string down the high school hallway as his "dog." It's thanks to this teacher that my Stanley, who has absolutely no interest in numbers, has decided that he might take physics, chemistry, or calculus after all.

So you see? Find the right teacher, and any subject becomes interesting.

⊞ ⊞ ⊞

But it doesn't always work. Stanley was telling me the other day that his idea of a good teacher is one who doesn't worry about students' self-esteem and who at the same time has high expectations. An image flashed into my mind. It was that of Stanley's most recent mid-term report, and next to his algebra teacher's name was the comment she had written: "Poor work habits. Not working up to abilities."

And so I said, "Well, Stanley, it doesn't sound like your algebra teacher is too worried about your self-esteem."

"Yeah, she's one of the good teachers."

"Well, if she's such a good teacher, why are you not doing so well in there?"

"Oh, she's a good teacher all right. I'm just not a good student."

So there you have it, folks, straight from the G/T kid's mouth. (He does get brownie points for being honest.) The old "They Gotta Wanna" principle plays out, even when the teacher is top notch like this one.

This is probably a good thing for a parent to remember before he or she goes charging into a parent/teacher conference with every intention of drawing and quartering the teacher because the student got her first "F" ever. Sometimes a G/T student finally gets a low grade because it was the first time she has been challenged to work harder and to stretch. If gifted kids aren't used to things like stretching or studying, doing homework, and keeping track of it, it's hard on them when they have to do it for the first time. After all, those things are so tedious. Up to now, they have been able to drift through their classes without really doing anything. So when they're suddenly faced with a teacher who holds them accountable, that teacher deserves kudos rather than judos. Parents should be alert to this.

I sat outside a classroom once during parent/teacher conference week and witnessed the unfortunate lambasting of a teacher. Since the parents made no effort at being discreet, I didn't feel that my eavesdropping was an issue. I'll call the two of them the

Glare Gang. They took turns clicking their tongues, shaking their heads in disgust, and informing the teacher that their son was truly brilliant and that she should know better than to even *think* about scoring him on his actual work, which, if he wasn't doing it, was probably her fault.

Funny. Just the previous year, my own son had this teacher and did equally as poorly. Fortunately, I'm quite aware of his work habits.

Then you have the other side of the coin. You have the teachers with the one-size-fits-all curriculum model, where we will all color inside the lines and all of the children will progress at the same rate and will be on the same page at the same time. It's the herding principle. Stay with the group. These teachers' expectations are mediocre and yet impossible. These are the teachers gifted kids endure. A book for this situation might be called *Survival: Darwin's Theory as Applied to Well-Behaved Children Who Don't Cause Any Trouble and Who Sit Nicely and Quietly and Memorize their Vocabulary Words.* The subtitle would be *Particularly Children Who Only Ask to Use the Lavatory When it Is Convenient for the Instructor.*

This book would be the bane of children everywhere.

⊞ ⊞ ⊞

Take the boy in kindergarten who was supposed to be practicing writing numbers 1 and 2 on his paper. When the aide came by to check on him, he had written only A, B, and HRF.

"What are you doing?" she asked, "Aren't you supposed to be working on your numbers?"

"Shh! These are my secret plans," he said.

"Oh, what are your secret plans?"

"Well, I've got Plan A and Plan B, and if they fall through, then there's Plan HRF."

"Wow," she said, "That's very impressive. What does it all mean?"

"I can't tell you. It's a secret."

What it really means is that, as far as he's concerned, whether he can count his plans or not is beside the point. He'd rather work on something more interesting than numbers 1 and 2. Sometimes it's torturous for a child to stay with the pack no matter how much he wants to please the teacher.

I haven't decided whether the color-in-the-lines teachers rank slightly ahead of or just behind the teachers who have no expectations at all. Perhaps it could be considered dead even.

While gifted kids—like any other kids—need to learn to follow the rules, they also need to learn that it's okay to be themselves and that it's okay to want to learn more and achieve more than what has been outlined in the lesson plan.

At our school the other day, one of the third-grade teachers let her class go out for a bathroom break. She told them that she expected them to come right back, so when it took longer than it should have and not one of them had returned, she went out to check on them.

She found them lined up neatly in the hallway. They were quiet and well-behaved and meek—most of them anyway. In the front of the line, giving orders, was a leadership-gifted little girl who felt that it was her personal responsibility to get those kids back to class safely, all in an orderly group, and without any fooling around.

She was just being herself.

❖ ❖ ❖

Another gifted little boy at a different school found himself in an agonizing situation in the school cafeteria. True, this is a common place to have agonizing situations, but this little boy was told that he couldn't leave the cafeteria to go out to play until he finished his chili. So being a good creative problem solver, he spooned the chili into his pockets, raised his hand to show his clean tray to the cafeteria warden, and left with a smiling face but a rather strange gait.

⊞ ⊞ ⊞

Being gifted is not an excuse for bad behavior, but it's important to remember that you're dealing with children who solve problems in non-traditional ways and who have non-traditional needs, and *sometimes* they deserve to be heard. I mean, perhaps the cafeteria warden should have cut the kid a little "slack" (Get it? Slacks, pants, pockets, chili? It's sort of a chain-reaction pun.) instead of insisting that every child should enjoy and appreciate the finer side of spicy beans.

I once read that many gifted children grow up to become janitors and housewives and other ordinary people. My grandfather was a very gifted man, and he was a terrific janitor. I'm proud of him. I am a housewife, and I see no shame in that.

Our concern should be that these children be given options and the opportunities to pursue whatever it is that they want to pursue, whatever career they want to enjoy. Too many times, gifted children are required to stifle their obsessions, their curiosities, their questions, all of the things that make them both weird and wonderful, and are told to sit quietly and wait for the rest of the class to catch up.

"Just do the worksheet, Junior. We don't need to make this complicated."

So Junior tunes out and does the worksheet, not because he sees any value in it, but because the tall guy standing in the front of the class told him to quit thinking so much, the thing that Junior does best, because when Junior thinks too much, it creates problems for everyone else.

Junior is no dummy, so he learns to survive in his environment. He learns not to raise his hand to ask a question, because one of the following four things is likely to happen: (1) the teacher will look at Junior and say, "Have you been daydreaming again? We just went over that. Class, would somebody please explain to Junior the difference between petals and leaves?" (2) the teacher will wonder how in the world Junior's question relates to the subject at hand, even though the connection is obvious in Junior's mind, and the teacher will ask Junior to please stay on task and focus on the current subject, (3) the teacher will not be able to answer Junior's question, because the teacher does not know the answer, or (4) Junior fears that he might ask a question with an embarrassing answer since he is never sure what is appropriate to ask.

I remember the time when I was fourteen and in a church class. I demanded to know what circumcision was. The teacher tried to put me off and told me to ask my parents to explain it to me. The boys in class were slightly uncomfortable. Whether that was due to the explanation I demanded or the thought of circumcision itself, I'm not sure.

I said, "Come on, how bad can it be? It's in the Bible, for Pete's sake." Obviously I had not read the Songs of Solomon.

Finally, I gave up. The teacher called my mother and asked her to explain it to me. I still didn't see why it was such a big deal. All I know is that my mom giggled through the entire discussion, and I had to keep saying, "No, really, just tell me what happens."

Then at the end I said, "Oh."

I learned to think twice after that about asking questions in class. And the Junior we recently discussed usually figures this out at a much earlier age. I'm just a slow learner.

Junior sometimes gives up on the questions and the pursuit of an education entirely, and he drops out, either mentally or physically. And if anyone goes to bat for him, there's a chance they could strike out before they even step up to the plate, because they aren't wearing the team shirt.

⊞ ⊞ ⊞

So how does a parent or a teacher campaign for gifted education without living in fear of being called an elitist?

You don't. You just have to live with the label, and you do it even though you know that being gifted is often a double whammy. Each gifted child is blessed and cursed at the same time. So you ignore the annoyed looks and you root for your son, the intellectual quarterback, because he's doing what he loves best and he's good at it. You make sure he has everything he needs to play the game and that he has a coach who believes in him.

You make sure he has his helmet on—with the opening in the front—and that his shirt is on right-side-out. And you yell to him to turn around when he's heading toward the wrong set of goal posts.

When all is said and done, if he gets drafted to a great team and opts out to become the water boy because that's what he's always wanted to do and that's what makes him happy, then you go along with that, too, and encourage him to succeed there.

And you gently remind him every now and then to carry the bucket with the open side up.

9: I Already Know How

This would be my daughter, Magnolia. She learned how to read with the rest of her class. Cool. But when I encouraged her to continue reading so that she could improve her skills, her reply was no, but thanks for asking. "Naw, I already know how to read," she said.

We are told that if we read to our children, they will be more likely to develop a love for reading themselves. I love reading so much, my husband tells me that if I bring home one more book, our house will tip over from all of the weight on the bookshelves in the library. I've tried to pass my love of reading on to my kids. Stanley used to be a reader, and Otto lives for reading. Pandora began pretending to read paperback novels when she was nine months old. And whenever I sit down on the couch, Rupert's eyes light up and he says, "Book?" Then he runs off to get a book before I change my mind.

But Magnolia never cared. Fortunately, last year when she was in third grade, she and I joined a mother-daughter book club. Every month we were assigned a different book which we were supposed to read together. They weren't Magnolia's kind of books, but somehow, after I read a few pages to her, she became somewhat more interested. A chapter or two later and she was even enjoying herself.

Then she got the funny idea into her head that it was possible that other books had something to offer. They might even be worth reading on her own.

You can't blame the girl for being reluctant to take on a book. Turning pages can be such a workout.

However, most of the time when a gifted child lacks motivation, it isn't as simple as the solution to Magnolia's lack of desire to read. All I had to do was pique her interest and open the door just wide enough to show her the possibilities that awaited her on the other side of the reading-is-boring wall.

Sometimes children lack motivation because a thing is difficult and they haven't learned to work or push themselves in an area outside of their obsessions. They're quick learners, and too often, one of the first things they learn is that it's easier to go with the flow than it is to work up to their ability. They discover early what the teacher's expectations are and that, usually, those expectations don't require the use of full brainpower. And so, being environmentally correct, they say, "Why waste my energy?"

Good enough is good enough. Unless they happen to run on the high-stress-level, perfectionist side of gifted. Then, nothing is ever good enough. In either case, the potential is there, but the motivation needs a tune-up.

Achieving an appropriate balance between work and leisure is a biggie when a kid is G/T. If she's an overachiever, then a parent or teacher needs to encourage her to slow down every once in a while and enjoy the fruits of her labors. If she's an underachiever, then she needs encouragement to quit eating fruit and get back to the fields.

Stanley is, at least in some areas, an underachiever. For example, when it comes to math, he has never done well, not because he can't, but because he doesn't have any reason to.

However, when Stanley was in seventh grade, he tested out of pre-algebra and skipped to the eighth-grade algebra class. At that point, he had a reason, a motivation. (He wanted to get out of a year's worth of work.) However, dealing with algebra was an entirely new experience for him. Math isn't in his interest area, nor is it one of his strong suits. For the first time in his entire school career, he was faced with assignments that challenged him. For the first time in his life, he had tears in his eyes as he struggled to understand an intellectual task. It was good for him. It helped him to have a little empathy for other kids who have to deal with that struggle on a daily basis. It was also good for him to have a chance to stretch his brain a bit, because it had developed a definite couch potato attitude.

Stanley probably gets his limited algebraic skills from me, his mother, but he must have gotten some from his father too, just a titch, because although he may struggle, he grasps, which is more than I could do. Algebra was an affliction for me. My instructors might as well have taught the whole class in Greek. It seemed to me that it was just some guy in front of the class who got excited about how X equals eight, if and only if Z is not greater than three times A, squared to the power of seven.

As far as I was concerned back then, letters and numbers don't mix. It was like taking a course where spelling crashed with math and left a horrible mess on the chalkboard—and there were no survivors. I used to think that it was an intelligence test similar to *The Emperor's New Clothes*. If you can see the sense in this mess, then you must be very easily fooled, you fool, because there is no sense to this mess.

I'm proud to say that I never once fell for the trick.

Actually, I wonder if I might have understood it better had it been taught differently. I mean, if someone told me that X was the murderer in a story, and the only clue that I had to go on was the fact that X was equivalent to a particular set of numbers, signs, and multitudinous other clues, I probably wouldn't have been able to put the book down until I had that thing solved. Just like the final guilty number, I would have had a motive— the satisfaction of solving a mystery. It's a matter of interest and creative problem-*giving*.

When I went to college, I remember calmly peeling the outer layer of chocolate off of a snack cake and thinking that life was so very good, while all my classmates were desperately cramming for finals. The tests were a cinch as far as I was

111

concerned. All you had to do was sit, listen to the professor's lectures, and maybe scan the textbook.

Notes? You take notes? Wimp!

I always aced the tests. Too bad I didn't do so well on my homework, like papers and things. I mean, homework was like, well, work. Who had time for that business?

But hey, who needs college anyway, right? And grades, they're just numbers and letters and all that stuff. They're just like algebra—they don't really mean anything. Not unless you want to get a good job or something, and maybe have an income that will support you eventually. For some kids, college is so much more about other things, like meeting people and joining organizations.

Recently, Stanley, the can-do kid who doesn't always "do" when it comes to report cards, brought home an A+ from a class. On the back of the report card was a lovely note about how wonderful Stanley was, how helpful, how the teacher loved having him in class. It was the first thing he showed me when I picked him up from school. He didn't just show me, he read aloud the note on the back. Then, when his dad got home, he read the note on the back to *him*. When one of his friends called, Stanley told him about the A+ and read the note to *him,* too.

After he'd run out of people to impress, he heaved a satisfactory sigh and said, "I think I'll put this up on the refrigerator."

Until then, I didn't know he cared.

When it came to taking the exam to get his learner's permit to drive, I thought he might care a bit more. He did study, he said. But to Stanley, studying implies that a person has read the title page and the subheading and verified that the knowledge in-between is beneath making the effort and is probably something he could just guess at anyway.

I said, "Are you sure you studied?"

He said, "Yeah, besides, even the kids at school who don't do well on their schoolwork pass this thing the first time. It'll be a cinch."

Uh huh. That explains why Stanley the Brilliant failed his driving exam the first time. That also explains why Stanley the Brilliant failed it the second time. I'm still waiting for the results of a third try. The good news is that he's decided that perhaps he ought to read beyond the subheadings this time and get to the humdrum little details such as how many feet before a turn one is supposed to begin signaling. I think his new interest in studying has something to do with having to cough up twenty dollars to pay for the second set of exams.

It's all right. It's not as though I'm in any hurry for Stanley to hit the road. In fact, I sort of wonder if the people at the DMV have heard about his incredible driving skills and are failing him on purpose. If this is the case, I, and the entire town for that matter, owe them a thank-you note.

⊞ ⊞ ⊞

Stanley has a history for studying only when it works to his advantage. And no, good grades alone do not convince him that the work is worth the effort. Sometimes, he actually believes that it would be in his best interest to fail.

Take the state spelling bee. He was in seventh grade and had taken first place at the county level. Spelling has always been his best area, or at least it was in first grade. Since then it has leveled off to match the expectations of various English teachers. He aims to please, especially if it means less work for him.

We received this booklet in the mail from the organizers of the state spelling bee. It was a study guide, with all of the words they planned to use for the contest. How can a kid go wrong when he has the list of words right there to study?

Easy. Don't open the book.

I tried to go over it with him, but there were approximately three million, four hundred eighty seven thousand words in that little booklet—okay, give or take a few. And just about every word in there was beyond pronunciation. Nonetheless, Stanley was perfectly capable if he were to put his mind to it.

But he didn't want to put his mind to it.

Now this is fine. Far be it from me to force my child into succeeding only to make me proud—though who am I to complain if it happens to work out that way sometimes? Hey, it all evens out in the end. I mean, I didn't disown him when he was out in left field counting clouds, did I? So maybe I wore dark sunglasses; I still gave him a ride home at the end of the game.

The real reason I pushed him to do well was because he wasn't about to make any effort of his own volition. Why? Duh, Mom, if he won at the state level, he'd have to miss the junior high talent show. And if he missed the junior high talent show, he and his band, the band that hadn't one song put together but was still going to wow the entire seventh and eighth grade student body, plus the faculty, with their sheer talent and soon afterward become an overnight national sensation, wouldn't be able to perform.

I said, "Uh, Stanley, if it's exposure you're looking for, don't you think being on national TV would be the best bet?"

"Mo-om," he said, so patiently. It was apparent to him that I had not thought things through. "Even if I am on national television, I'm only going to be spelling. It's not like I'm going to get an acting contract or get hired for a band because I know how to spell a word right. Like some talent scout is going to look at me and say, 'Wow, that kid spells with personality!'"

"Stanley, you never know what could happen. If you have an opportunity, you should take it and make the most of it. It's not like this is going to happen every day, you know. And you can always play for your school some other time, like after you've practiced a little more."

But since I'm only the mom in this picture, he said, "No thanks. I know what I'm doing."

So he took seventh place at the state bee by not studying. We sat there for hours cheering him on, praying for him every time he stood up to spell a word. Other kids looked nervous. Some looked confident. But Stanley just sort of meandered up to the microphone, spelled the word as if he were yawning, and then sat back down in his chair. Well, maybe "sat" is stretching it a bit. Stanley never sits. He slumps. He's a very comfortable kind of person. If he were Ruler of the World, his first edict would be to do away with all straight-backed chairs and replace them with recliners or bean bags.

The point is, Stanley wasn't nervous because he wasn't trying to win. He was probably sitting up on the stage mentally practicing his guitar chords. When he finally got a word wrong, he was okay with that. After all, he knew that we would still take him out for dinner afterwards.

I said, "Stanley, you did great, but just think of what you could have done if you had studied the words."

"Oh well," he said.

Shortly after that experience, I ran across a news article about the girl who had won the national spelling bee the year before.

With great pleasure, I saved it and showed it to Stanley.

"Wow, she got on the *David Letterman Show*!" he said.

"Yep. I guess her personality showed through, even though she was doing nothing more than spelling a word on national television."

The icing on the cake was when the junior high talent show was canceled.

My husband tells me that I have a problem with gloating. I say, however, that when you're a mom, gloating rules! Besides, on the occasions that I *am* right, I've got to get all of the credit I can. It doesn't happen that often.

🏶 🏶 🏶

There is another reason that gifted, talented children might lack motivation to learn new things. Sometimes they think that they already know everything. It's a matter of pride. Knowing things is what they're good at.

Case Study: Two grown men, namely my husband the business man and my brother-in-law, Ignatius, the engineer, decided that since it was the hottest summer on record, the smart thing to do was to build a swimming pool. My husband's priority was to do this cheaply, while Ignatius's priority was to build something with structural integrity. I offered a solution to both of their problems: buy an above-ground pool kit for around one hundred fifty dollars, put it together in the back yard, and then—and this is the complicated part—place the hose in the pool to fill it up. But no. The dynamic duo decided that a kit would be beneath them. They would build a better and cheaper pool, by Jove.

After much analysis and purchasing of supplies (and a few minor experimental catastrophes), we became the proud owners of an almost coffin-like, octagon of a wooden pool, reinforced with beams extending from the sides into poles that had been anchored in cement. Two giant tarps were draped over and inside the structure to hold the water. It looked like a giant, wooden tarantula with a blue back.

And all this creative genius set us back an easy four hundred dollars.

I'll have to admit, though, it *did* work, even if there was no easy way to get in or out.

When I hear the phrase, "that idea doesn't hold water," it means more to me than it does to most people.

Yes, you may use this story to scare your children if you find that they *think* they know more than they really do. "Once upon a time, there were two men with college degrees...."

There is a satisfaction in knowing things. For example, I feel a great deal of satisfaction in knowing that I was right about the pool.

But just *knowing* things isn't enough. Understanding why something is true, justifying what you know, and using high-level thinking rather than high-level memorizing should be a priority. It is the nature of the gifted individual to question things, and that natural tendency alone should be enough to encourage them to think and not take things for granted. But they can get lazy, especially if they're in a hurry to move on to the next thought. And they can get in the habit of trusting their sources.

When I was a sophomore in high school, it was an election year, and I knew exactly how my dad was going to vote. There was one candidate that he absolutely couldn't stand, and because I had a great deal of respect for my dad's opinions, I mentioned that, if I were old enough to vote, I wouldn't vote for that guy either.

My dad asked, "Why do you say that?"

"I don't know. I guess because you aren't going to vote for him."

Then my dad said, "Don't you *ever* vote the way somebody else does. You have to know *why*. You have to know for yourself."

I gained even more respect for my dad after he said that. It struck me that he was more worried about my ability to reason and think for myself than he was about my undying loyalty to his opinions. He didn't want to raise an obedient cookie-cutter product; he wanted to raise an individual who didn't stop thinking and didn't stop questioning.

In the movie, *I.Q.*, one of the characters says a line that I love: "Question everything." It's a simple idea with high-potential possibilities.

Think. Analyze. Evaluate.

It's also the difference between bright and gifted students—though sometimes the only thing a gifted child questions is the notion that a test is worth the heavy pencil lifting.

And while it's true that not every kid is going to love every subject enough to cut it into tiny pieces and then consume it with ravishing hunger, the situation can still be improved.

There are three things that contribute to a child's motivation: (1) we tell them we believe that they *do* have the ability to achieve and accomplish, (2) we let them know that we have high expectations, and (3) then we challenge them.

When Otto began seventh grade, he didn't care much for algebra. He'd received several F's for work either not finished or not turned in. He said he was bored. I spoke with the counselor about this, and she in turn spoke with his teacher. His algebra teacher began giving Otto more attention in class and offering him some interesting personal challenges. She let him know that she knew he was smart and that she expected him to rise to those challenges.

His attitude changed. He did all of the extra credit he could get his hands on and pulled an A+ out of the class that quarter. He has loved algebra ever since.

Motivation from an outside source is often the beginning of motivation from within. I told Magnolia that she was going to sit down and read that book with me whether she liked it or not. I can do that because I'm the Mom, and I can see that she hasn't given this reading business a fair shot. I also can see that it's going to have an effect on her ability to get along in the civilized world later.

I say, "Listen, kid, you don't have to grow up to be a librarian, but you *are* going to improve your reading skills."

And she begrudgingly picks up the book and pouts through the first two chapters.

Then I pull my favorite trick, which is to say, "Oops, it's getting late. We'd better stop for tonight." Because just about that time, Magnolia is whetting her appetite for more story. I know that if I continue without her admitting that it's something she wants, she'll say that she only read the book under duress. But if it's her choice to continue, if she insists upon it, then she'll recognize where the motivation is coming from. I hand the opportunity to her all garnished and on a platter, but she's the one who takes the second helpings.

Parents spend a lot of time worrying about how to motivate their kids. I know that I do, anyway. But then I look back at my own life, and I relax a little.

I was not a highly motivated student. The last semester of my senior year in high school, instead of AP classes, I took three hours of art, two hours of drama, and one hour of psychology. When it came to careers, I had narrowed the field down to: (1) anything that had to do with art, (2) made a lot of money, and (3) wasn't boring. Of course, I also wanted to be beautiful and well-liked.

Since fashion modeling required a certain amount of coordination and grace, I chose to go into the next best thing: fashion design.

Then, after only one year of college, I got married. My aspirations suddenly changed from becoming a glamorous fashion designer with her own label to becoming a mother—and a stay-at-home mom at that.

I don't think that I ever honestly wanted to become a fashion designer. It required too much work to achieve a goal that I was never one hundred percent sold on. So I dropped out of college, much to everyone's disappointment, and worked to help get my hubby through college. I was told I would regret my decision—not the mommy decision, but the dropping out of college decision.

And I did. Only now I don't. Sure, I'd love to go back to college, and I used to kick myself for not finishing when I had the chance. But then I realized that if I had continued in college, I would have continued to pursue a goal I never really cared about. And if I'd kept my eyes on that goal, I might have missed out on the one thing, other than being a mom, that I felt truly compelled to do.

I didn't know that I was going to be a writer until after my third child was born. English and composition had always been a breeze for me in school, but it didn't dawn on me that either one could bring fulfillment in my life. I guess what I'm saying is that it took me a long time to decide what I wanted to be when I grew up.

And when the realization hit me, it was the first time that I felt motivated enough to work hard at something that seemed at first impossible to achieve. It was the first time that I was willing to study and learn and be patient. It was the first time I was brave enough or strong enough to endure boatloads of rejection and criticism and glean the good from it.

I didn't know this—I couldn't know this—in high school when I was filling out the applications for college. At that point, I was just going through the motions and doing what was expected of me.

People are not like plants that grow neatly in a row. Yes, they all need food, sun, and water, but they don't always bloom in season, and they don't always come in seed packets with beautiful color photographs of what they're going to look like when they finally mature.

So when I look at my kids, and they're not progressing at the standard rate, I tell myself that it's okay. The best motivations can be encouraged, but they can't be rushed. Sometimes people have to learn things about themselves before they can comprehend the importance of whatever it is that they need to do with their lives.

I do still try to keep working on that motivation problem, but the goal isn't the traditional worldly version of success, though that might be a nice bonus, and I'm not one to turn it away.

The way I see it, I have three goals for my children to be accomplished as soon as possible, but we'll wait if they need more time to figure things out. What other choice do we have?

The first goal is to have integrity, to be true to themselves at all times. The second goal is that they be able to support themselves so that they can respect and feel good about who they are. Supporting themselves means that they are able to hold down a job—any job—as long as it meets whatever their bare necessities are. It means that they have self-respect. Then the third goal is joy. I want them to be happy, which I think is a by-product of integrity and self-respect.

It's really pretty simple. Sure, I hammer on them about grades and college and sitting up straight. And I do everything I can think of to light a fire in them to aspire to whatever great things they are capable of accomplishing. That's my job. But if I can see them happy, then *that* will be my privilege.

In Ayn Rand's *The Fountainhead*, there are two characters—Howard Roark, a man who is highly motivated and true to himself from the beginning, and Peter Keating, also highly motivated and out to impress the world, even if it means leaving himself behind. There is one part in that book that touched me deeply. After years of selling out to the world, Peter decides to go back to his art, the thing he loves most but has sacrificed. He brings a painting to show Howard, because he knows Howard will be honest with him. But when Howard looks at the picture, Peter knows that it's too late. He's lost what talent he possessed. He's wasted his life with distractions.

I cried when I read that part. No, I sobbed.

Because it's really sad to see someone lose himself. However, I believe that if something can be lost, it can also be found.

Motivation—the good kind, not the bad kind—is where it's at.

🔡 🔡 🔡

The bad kind of motivation is the kind that stresses you out. It's the urgent need to please everyone else. Some gifted kids have a tendency to get caught up in the web of perfectionism. It can be a trap, where if they make one mistake, they feel as though they've lost everything. They've failed. They get depressed, discouraged, and want to give up, call it quits. They forget about all of the good things that they are and focus primarily on what they aren't.

If that's the case for a child you know, question the motivation. Is what they're doing going to lead to happiness? What are they willing to sacrifice to achieve a picture-perfect intellect? Who are they trying to impress? Why? Why? Why?

Don't give them the answers. Let them figure it out for themselves. And don't tell them it's a test, or they'll sacrifice honesty for a good score.

▦ ▦ ▦

It's difficult to find the balance between pushing your kids to do better, and pushing them to a total Type A personality. But let's say you're a mother bird. Those little babies are going to have to get out of the nest and fly on their own. If you harp, or let's say chirp, about it too much, going on and on about how the Jones' chicks flew three days ago, and why haven't your own brood done as well, and how important it is to fly with elegance and refinement and not bring shame to the family nest, then those babies of yours are not going to enjoy flying. They might do it mostly to get away from your chirping, but they won't enjoy it. However, if you tell them that you know they'll do it when they're ready because you have all of the faith in the world in them, and you nudge them a bit, maybe challenge them to go stand on the edge of the nest and encourage them to try a couple of wing flaps, and you fly about a bit yourself, and do a loop-de-loop just to show them how much fun it is and the independent feeling of it all, then your babies will be more likely to soar, mentally as well as physically.

If that doesn't work, you can do what some parents have tried. If you can at least get them to stand at the edge of the nest, maybe you can give them a small push accompanied by an "Oops. Dear me. How did that happen?" Because those babies have got to learn how to fly if they are going to survive.

Besides, once they start flying and get out on their own, you can turn their bedroom into that office or sewing or exercise room you've always wanted.

Motivation.

10: I Gotta Be Me

Any time a student in our local school system is identified, the G/T specialist will sit down with the proud new parents and give them a training manual or other information about gifted children. Not a training manual for the child, but for the parent. One of the items that is almost always included is a list of some of the common characteristics of gifted children.

It's handy to have it all boiled down to a list like that, but it's important to remember that each item on the list has a wide range of possibilities. Let's take a quick run through some of them.

Gifted children are supposed to experience *higher levels of sensitivity*. This includes all kinds of sensitivity, including sound, smell, and taste. Pandora can smell flowers in a perfume factory. The girl has such a highly developed sense of smell that it's embarrassing. Thankfully, she's learned that it isn't polite to mention everything that one can smell, especially around company. She also went through a stage when she was a toddler where she wouldn't go to sleep unless there were no wrinkles in her blanket. I had to drape her blanket over her and then smooth it out or she would scream until I came back to fix it. Then she would point at the offending crease or creases and look at me as though I had better get it right this time or else.

Another girl I know, Agnes, had to have the seams on her socks aligned exactly along the tops of her toes or she would complain that the socks hurt her feet. Her shoelaces had to be tied in perfectly matching bows, with the loops even and each lace end hanging the same length. The tags on the back of her clothing irritated her, and she became so particular and fussy that her mother ended up hiding all of her clothes, except for two outfits which she alternated wearing every day to kindergarten. Even her hair bothered her enough that her mother, to save her own sanity, had to cut Agnes's hair short.

Talk about a high maintenance kid.

For Otto, being sensitive applies to other people as well, but it mainly means that he is touchy about whether other people treat him fairly or not. He's also touchy in the likes-hugs-and-back-scratches way, and he often comes up and puts his arm around me—though I think he enjoys putting his arm around me mostly to emphasize his height and the idea that I can't see anything above his chin when he is that close.

Stanley's sensitivities involve food and textures. Anything soggy makes him gag. He can't eat milk on his cereal. He can't eat cold leftover noodles or he'll throw up. He can't even *touch* anything soggy. I asked him to pick up one of Rupert's stray Crunchy Wunchies one morning.

"I can't, Mom, it's too gross."

"Stanley, it's a piece of cereal."

"But it's *wet!*" By this time, his face was green.

"Stanley, you are probably going to have kids some day, and you are going to need to know how to pick up a piece of wet cereal. Now, cowboy up and take care if it, please."

"All right," he said, but he had to avert his eyes as he picked up the slimy circle from off the floor. It was a very dramatic situation. In Act Three, he miraculously managed to get the cereal all of the way to the garbage can without becoming physically ill.

I was so proud of him. "Thank you, Stanley."

He then exited stage left before Rupert could drop another Crunchy Wunchy.

Stanley is also emotionally sensitive. When he was about three years old, our family went through a traumatic divorce (as though there is such a thing as a non-traumatic divorce). The whole situation affected him of course. He was sensitive to every signal that somebody was about to leave. He loved movies, but he cried if someone said goodbye in them or if anything remotely sad happened. You couldn't even swat flies around Stanley. He has recovered from this for the most part, though he still suffers heartbreak over the whole situation and probably always will.

I did note some progress in his emotional state when he was five. We were watching the movie *White Fang* when the mother wolf died and left her young pup alone in the wilderness. I thought, "This is just terrific. Now he's going to be devastated all over again."

But with his amazing and endearing ability to rebound from tragedy, he piped up, "Wow, now he can do whatever he wants!" It warmed my heart.

Even though I remarried when Stanley was four, and Stanley thinks of my husband as his dad, he is still heartbroken about the divorce and misses his first dad. He wants to see him and talk to him often. When Stanley was in sixth grade and had to write an autobiography for school, he mentioned the divorce and how painful it was for him. He tells me now, four years after the autobiography, that he's decided that it's just the way things are, and he's going to have to get over it, but it will be easier said than done.

The experience has instilled in him a strong desire to always be a part of a family, even though belonging to a family and sharing and getting along is not the easiest thing to do. He tells me he thinks we should have five more children. Thank goodness he has no say in the matter.

It is typical for gifted children and adults to be extra-sensitive emotionally. They take things seriously. I remember as a child when I was in the car with my mom driving, and she hit a dog and killed it. She isn't a dog person, but the thought of being responsible for the pain and agony and death of that dog upset her greatly. In fact, she pulled off to the side of the road and became almost hysterical at the thought of what she had done.

She finally gathered herself together enough to locate the owners of the dog and inform them of the dog's death. She was probably more upset about the whole thing than the owners were.

And I mentioned earlier that she has been known to cry when she gets pulled over for a speeding ticket. It causes her emotional pain just to think she has done something wrong.

Besides sensitivity, a *keen sense of justice* seems to be a universal characteristic for gifted kids—at least it does when I look at my own small sampling of children. They all love justice, particularly if they can pin the blame on one of their siblings and have him or her pay the price. Justice is also one of the reasons that they ask "Why?" when you tell them to do or not to do something. They want to hear your reasons, because they want to decide if your reasons are fair and just before they decide whether or not they will comply.

I've had to inform my children that they shouldn't expect fair treatment, because I am going to try and give each child what that particular child needs, not what an older or younger sibling needs and gets. This includes consequences as well as rewards. Each child is different, and I want them to realize and appreciate that fact rather than hollering, "Hey, that's not fair. You didn't do that for me!"

I also tell them that life isn't fair. If it were, they would probably be a lot worse off than they are now, because in a lot of ways, they're very lucky kids.

Next on the list is *perfectionism.* Ha! Cross that one off my list. Any perfectionist traits have so far been mild. Wait, upon further introspection, it occurs to me that they *do* expect other people to be perfect. They are idealists when it comes to someone *else's* behavior.

You can have fun with perfectionists. When my sister Hortense used to baby-sit for four-year-old Alfred, he would align his cars in a perfect formation, and it would drive him crazy if something should happen to mess it up. So of course,

Hortense would move one of the cars just a titch, and Alfred would discover it and move the car back. She would then sneak over and move a car again, and he would put it back. This was repeated until Hortense became distracted by something else, like maybe his parents coming home. Cruel? Yes. But try it. It's a great rainy day activity.

Intensity. Hmm. Okay, yes, they can get intense. Stanley is usually listening intently to the radio. And he used to be intent on those letters (the good old days). Otto's determination, when he so chooses to exercise it, goes beyond intense.

Pandora is intent on looking at the mummy book and on picking up any information she can get her hands on. She especially loves learning new terms and phrases. She built a tent the other day with an extension coming off one side. Sadly, Rupert wasn't nearly as impressed with the architecture and decided to pull the extension down. Pandora yelled, "Mom! Rupert just destroyed the west wing of my tent!"

I have no idea where she picked up the term "west wing." I don't believe it came from the TV series, because we have no cable, umbilical cord, or satellite dish connected to our home. This is mostly for my sake. If we had any kind of reception at all, I would be watching right now rather than writing. This book would never have seen the light of day.

Pandora has a knack for knowing just how and when to use her new terms, too. And she prefers to save the new swear words for loud expression in public places, thank you very much.

Pandora is also intense when it comes to her activities. She could play with Legos® all day long without a break. I often have to go downstairs and check on her just to make sure she is still alive and well. If she enjoys something, it will continue to receive her full attention until an outside force pulls her away.

Magnolia is intent on getting everything she wants and intent on getting out of everything that she doesn't want to do. My next book will be titled *One Hundred Different Ways to Ask*

Your Mother the Same Question and will be subtitled *Even though You'll Get the Same Answer Every Time.* Whenever you feel like becoming annoyed, you can open up the book to any page, pick a question, and then slam the book shut while you say, "I said 'no,' and I meant 'no'!" Parent therapy. It's also good for birth control.

Naturally curious? Yes. My children especially like asking questions for which I have no answer. However, I was greatly relieved when my husband sat down with Stanley to have that little father-son talk about life in general and how it comes about. "How much do you know?" he asked Stanley.

Stanley, who was twelve at the time, said, "I know enough to know that I don't want to know anymore."

Hold that thought, Stanley.

High energy. Wait, this one is a joke, yes? No? Well then, how come Stanley missed out on it entirely? How come the kid can't stand up straight and has to bend so far over the table that his face is three inches away from and parallel to his plate?

Actually, Magnolia is a high-energy child, but it comes and goes with her mood. She is excited and enthusiastic when things are going her way. She wants to be involved in everything and go everywhere. Can she go to work with her dad? Can she go to the store with me? Can we go for a walk? Can she make cookies? Can she throw a party for her friends? Can she decorate the house? Why am I upset about the gallon of confetti that she cut from colored paper and then threw all over the living room floor? But when she has to do something painful, like vacuum all of that confetti up, suddenly she doesn't feel well. She's tired. She wants a nap.

Otto is high energy as well. While Stanley can't make it up or down the stairway without slipping into a reverie, Otto can't make it across the floor without intentionally falling or practicing a slide kick. And as Otto is now six feet tall, his high energy can be tough on the house.

Acute self awareness. My children are very aware of themselves. They are also very aware when there is only one piece of cake left.

Pandora is very aware of her body. She wants to know all about it, but she has a particular fascination with growing "bumps." Bumps are what women use to feed their babies with. Yes, in our home, we pride ourselves on using accurate and scientific terminology. Anyway, Pandora has a toy dog that makes slurping sounds when its nose is next to it's doggy dish. The other day, I heard the slurping sounds and turned around to see Pandora with the dog dish under her shirt where bumps would normally be located. She was nursing her dog.

Talkative? Yes. Stanley talks about movies and rock bands. He tells me more than I ever wanted to know and then some. I try to remind him that I don't want to hear about movies that I haven't seen, and that I'd much rather hear him talk about himself or what's happening in his life, because he's a lot more interesting to me than any rock star might be.

Otto insists on telling me about every task, every event, every algebra problem, in a painstaking, step-by-step conversation. "First I wrote down the equation on my paper, but then I realized that I had accidentally written down a two instead of a five, so I had to erase it. And then my pencil fell on the floor, but I picked it up and crossed out the sixes because they canceled each other out...." You get the idea. I try to be patient and listen to my children, but sometimes with Otto I grit my teeth and try not to yell, "What? What's the point? Get on with it, man!" I tell him too, that I'm not so interested in algebra as I am in his life. I forget that, at least at that moment, algebra *is* his life.

As for Magnolia, she loves to talk about anything, particularly her personal life, but anything will work, just so long as she can put off doing her chores. She usually comes up with at least fifteen I-have-to-tell-you-now-it's-really-important emergency conversations every day after school when she is supposed to be getting her jobs and her homework done. The thing that amazes me is that the really and truly important stuff is forgotten along with all of those announcements that they send home from school.

I don't know whose idea it was to send information home in the backpacks of children. If the schools want to communicate with parents, there has to be a better way. Even smoke signals would have a higher success rate.

Pandora talks about death and dreams and bodily functions. She also wants every last thing explained to her, whether it's an explanation telling her when it's proper to use the word "shall" or explanations of moral dilemmas and philosophical questions.

Busy mind that may lead to disorganization or non-task completion. Boy, do we have that one covered.

A need to understand? Uh huh. Well, maybe not a need to understand—more of a need to stall. The most commonly used word in our house is "Why?" Even Rupert knows this word. He may not understand what it means, but he realizes that it is our family's protocol to ask "Why?" every time I tell him to do something.

He also understands that the proper response to the question "What are you doing?" is "Nothing."

Exceptional reasoning ability. This one is optional. The kids will have it when they want it bad enough. When Pandora was about twelve months old, she figured out how to climb out of her crib. But she took it a step farther. She reasoned that falling from her crib could be a painful process, so she threw her blankets on the floor first and made a landing pad.

Noncomformity. Stanley is the epitome of the word. No, he doesn't have fluorescent spiked hair or a navel piercing. Those things are too run-of-the-mill for a guy like him. However, a three-piece suit made entirely out of fake fur? Yeah, that sounds about right. But being the prude that I am, I have limited him to one pair of fake fur pants. And when he sits with one knee crossed over the other one in a dainty manner and I tell him that he might want to rethink that or some of the other boys might make fun of him, he says, "I don't care. I'm comfortable."

Otto doesn't go out of his way to be different, but neither does he go out of his way to fit in. He doesn't want to be like everyone else, but he's not going to stay up nights figuring out how best to prove it.

Magnolia, the beautiful, loves trends. What? A new Whizmo to collect? Way cool! She's a marketer's dream. But then again, when you least expect it, she also goes her own way. Her sense of values has a tendency to outweigh her taste for the au currant.

As for Pandora, I have no idea what she will do when she hits school. She's very aware of everything and is exceptionally sensitive. She often tells me that I shouldn't wear my hair a certain way because other people will laugh at me and make fun of me. I just tell her that I'm used to it.

Pandora used to not care a fig about what anyone else thought about her. When she was three, she went through an anti-social stage where she growled at everyone. She didn't just growl when they looked at her wrong. No, she actually went out of her way to grab a stranger's attention to scowl and growl at them. When anyone made the mistake of saying, "What a *cute* little girl you have," she really let them have it, both barrels.

I'm hoping to resurrect this trait of Pandora's right about the time she's old enough to date. I'll put a "Beware of Pandora" sign on our front gate.

Questions rules and authority? Oh, yes. This one is unanimous, too, especially *my* rules and authority.

Vivid imagination? Check. I think every one of my children spends at least half of his or her day in a fantasy world. Pandora couldn't settle for having an imaginary friend; she had to *be* one. I heard about another boy, however, who is exceptionally gifted yet seems to have no imagination whatsoever. He has improved his abilities with time. Recently, when asked to rewrite the title for an essay in his own words, he changed "The Native Americans and The West" to "The West and The Native Americans." It was a very stressful transition for him.

▦ ▦ ▦

The key to translating the list of gifted characteristics is to recognize that each kid, while demonstrating those characteristics in different proportions and extremes, will vary from that list and will still maintain his or her uniqueness. Uniqueness is extremely important to them, generally speaking, except for those unique ones who would rather not be unique.

I look at each of my family members, brothers and sisters in turn, and it amazes me how different we are. We each had different struggles, struggles because of giftedness, different strengths, strengths because of giftedness, and different areas of success, success because of giftedness.

I look at my mother and her family. She has three sisters and a brother. Again, all different, again all gifted. None of them have handled it the same way.

I look at my children. There's Stanley, the social misfit who fits in so well socially because he isn't afraid to be himself. In fact, he glories in it—as well he should. He's also the one who continues to nominate himself for things like homecoming prince and sophomore class president. He won the presidency but missed the royalty. There's Otto, the tall, good-looking, more serious guy who could easily fit in but isn't sure if he wants to because that might mean crowds and pressure. There's Magnolia, the socially excited, socially aware, socially involved one, yet she's wise enough to be able to stand back, see how the game is played, and decide that she would rather play by her own rules. There's Pandora, who is like an old woman in a five-year-old body and is deeper than a five-year-old should be allowed to be. Then there's Rupert, who is blonde to every one else's brown, who laughs a lot, and whose face epitomizes the expression of someone who is glad to be alive, awake, and well-fed.

All of them struggle in one way or another with who they are. They have one thing in common, though. They don't want to be forced into being someone else. They want the freedom and acceptance of who they are and what they are capable of doing. No, they want more than that. They want recognition. They want to know who and what they are, and they want to know that who and what they are is a good thing to be. Because being intellectually gifted is one of the few gifts that come with a curse.

For some reason in our society, our schools in particular, it's okay if you want to be a better-than-average painter, it's okay if you want to be a better-than average runner, and it's okay if you want to be a better-than-average singer. Accomplish! Achieve! Use your gifts. Be the best you that you can be!

But don't be a better-than-average thinker. That scares some people.

Go ahead and get good grades and score well on standardized tests. That's okay. But don't think outside of the parameters. Doesn't matter if that's what you're good at. Society is uncomfortable with oddballs. It doesn't know what to do with them, what slot they fit into.

You can march to a different drummer, but only if everyone else can hear the drum. If you're wearing headphones or if you're "singing in your brain," you're out of luck.

Several years ago, I read about an interview with the actor Jeff Goldblum. I believe he was asked what he thought had made him successful. His reply was that his father had told him to always keep his eyes on his own paper.

That struck me as nothing less than brilliant. "Keep your eyes on your own paper." Don't worry about what, why, or how someone else is going about their life. Don't worry about whether or not you or your child fit the mold or fit the list of characteristics in the same way other gifted children do. Make your own mold and break it. It's okay.

That list of characteristics is helpful. It may help a teacher or an adult to be more aware of a child's individual needs, but it is not a checklist that is meant to be scored. It's not like one of those tests that you'll find in a women's magazine where you add up all of the multiple choice answers to discover your hidden personality and what perfume you should be wearing to match with it.

Most of the time, I have a pretty good sense of who I am, but I struggle here and there. I've tried to define myself, but there are too many contradictions in my personality, as well as too many changes that are constantly taking place. I've come to the conclusion that there is no definition of myself except for the single word: "Me."

My kids each have their own "Me," and all I can do is find out more about who they are and who they are becoming.

So I take the list and I check it twice, and maybe, instead of deciding to look for similarities in my kids, I decide to look for differences, because that's what makes them so cool.

It's like the old Arby's slogan: "Different is good."

And if you can't trust a fast-food slogan, well, what else is there?

Different *is* good.

11: Brain Food

My family has excelled in many areas; most of them we don't talk about in public. However, when we sit around the table together, we are merciless.

Our best moments have taken place in the kitchen.

You've heard of the saying "Too many cooks spoil the broth"? Well, guess what? When you're gifted, it only takes one.

Stanley is famous for his mac and cheese soup. "Oh, you mean I was supposed to drain the water *before* I put the cheese stuff in? I thought it didn't quite look right."

Magnolia's biggest kitchen achievement to date is her famous, soon-to-be-patented chocolate chip cookies. She said she could handle the task on her own. I almost believed her, but not quite. I checked on her every few minutes, but by the time she got to the last ingredient, the flour, I thought she was home free. She said the batter was still runny, so I told her to add more flour. However, even after a healthy addition of more flour, the batter sat in the bowl all glossy, and even-surfaced like a tureen of soup. Never believe a bowl of cookie dough. It can be so deceptive. When I stuck in the wooden spoon to stir it up a bit, the spoon penetrated the surface only to become a permanent fixture. It was a chocolate chip tar pit.

Using my exceptionally brilliant intuition that something had gone wrong, I began to look for clues. I didn't have to look too far before I saw a guilty looking plastic tub on the countertop.

"Uh, Magnolia? How much flour did you put in?"

135

"Seven-and-a-half cups."

"Did you get it out of that tub by any chance?"

"Yep."

"You didn't know that was powdered milk?"

"Powdered milk?"

So we added a little flour, not much, because the stirring would have required a steel-reinforced oar and both of Hulk Hogan's biceps, but we did our best, and then we crossed our fingers and dumped the entire mess onto a cookie sheet and baked it.

The kids enjoyed it. I told them they didn't need milk, just a glass of water to swirl the cookies around in.

A cookie a day keeps osteoporosis away.

My sister Edna doesn't cook much, but she does warm yogurt up in the microwave. If nobody is watching her carefully, she is capable of licking cream cheese frosting off an entire sheet cake and leaving nothing but a thin layer of glaze. Oh, and have you ever tried to stir up that lump of frozen orange juice? It can be a small tribulation for most people, but not for Edna. She'll stick her arm in the pitcher up to her elbow, and using her fist and her fingers, she'll squish that clump of concentrate into oblivion.

We rarely eat at her house.

My sister Darleen wins the prize for cake decorating. I mean, hey, if a chocolate cake won't come out of the pan in one piece, you can just scrape it out into a pile on a plate and mold it into volcano form. Drizzle a little red lava frosting over the top and you have a masterpiece.

When it comes to things made in the kitchen, I'm not merely a cook, I'm an artiste. Oh sure, I started off small and simple at age six by sneaking leftover turkey from Thanksgiving dinner and hanging it in my room to dry. Hey, it was as close as I could get to dried jerky, which was way out of my six-year-old budget. A bit later, I can't say that I'm particularly proud of the water-and-hard-boiled-egg-yoke mush I used to make with my

Easter eggs when I was seven. But let me tell you, those were just the seeds of an incredible talent yet to be unleashed. As I grew and matured, my genius grew with me. In my early married years, when someone asked me to bring finger food to a Halloween party, I brought real *finger* food. I took a slices of wafer-thin lunch meat, spread with a thin layer of cream cheese, and wrapped each of them around a piece of green onion. Then I scrunched up the lunch meat to make wrinkles around the bendy finger areas. I took food coloring and painted brown fingernails on one end and a red bloody stub on the other. Little toy rings lent the fingers a final semblance of authenticity. The best part is when someone bites into one of the fingers and the green onion inside crunches like a bone.

Are you impressed? Well, that's nothing. You should see my eyeballs on crackers.

And I can fake people out by making perfect imitations of ketchup, mustard, and mayonnaise—right down to the texture—with frosting. One of these days I'll be brave, or bored, and I'll serve them in the appropriate containers at a barbecue.

What's the use of all of this, you might ask?

Just that normal can be so mundane.

My road to success has been paved with failures as well. For example, when I was a kid and I was home alone, I tried to make glass out of molten sugar. It might not have been so bad if I hadn't tried to pour the seething substance into a plastic butter dish. I learned that melted plastic doesn't exactly scrub easily off the countertop.

My most memorable failure turned out to be a serendipitous success. I must warn you, this next story is rather graphic. If you are easily offended, perhaps you should plug your ears while you read it.

As usual, this experiment took place while my parents were gone and I had free rein of the kitchen. I was making chocolate pudding in the microwave for Myron and me. It wasn't the store-bought, boxed pudding. Anyone could do that. No, this was my own recipe. A little sugar, milk, cocoa, and cornstarch. Cook it in the microwave, stir occasionally, then cook it some more. Watch out, Betty Crocker!

I called Myron in to share the pudding with me, but he took one look at the warm, lumpy, brown mess and said he wasn't eating it. To emphasize his point, he scooped up a handful of pudding and flung it on the wall. He can be so subtle.

He then went back to watch his television show. I, of course, was appalled. I told him that there was no way that I was going to clean that mess up, and boy would he be in trouble when Mom and Dad got home. But he didn't give a care either way and went back to watching his television show.

About an hour's worth of fuming later, I gave in. After all, I was the oldest child; I was in charge. If there was a mess on the wall, I would be the one to hear about it. But when I went to clean it, it wasn't wipe-able. It *was* peel-able, so I proceeded to peel. I was then holding in my hand a rubbery, shiny, lumpy, dark brown mass that looked very similar to something that is generally only found in outhouses or bathrooms.

I suddenly forgot how angry I was with my brother and ran to show him my prize.

His eyes lit up when he saw it. "Give it to me. I have an idea."

Knowing that his powers of mischief were not to be doubted, I handed him the lump. He brought it upstairs into the bathroom and set it carefully on the toilet seat.

He had a look on his face, a glowing look. It was an "I'm in my element doing what I love to do best. Ain't life grand?" look.

"Watch this," he said.

Then he proceeded to wake up our four younger sisters and line them up in the bathroom. He pointed sternly at the offending lump and said, "All right. Who did this? Someone's going to be in big trouble when Mom and Dad get home!"

Each one of the girls looked guilty and panic-stricken at the same time. Fingers pointed. Accusations flew.

"Darleen did that. I saw her!"

"No, Gertrude did it. She does it all the time!"

"I didn't do anything!"

"It was Edna!"

"It was her, she never wipes!"

"It was Hortense!"

"It wasn't me!"

Myron went on. "Well, who's going to clean it up?"

The accusations began all over again until Myron was satisfied and sent them all back to bed. I'm sure they must have stayed awake in bed for a good hour, whispering allegations across the dark bedroom, shoring up their support wherever they could find it. I'm surprised that no one in my family ever went into politics.

This was only the beginning of a long and illustrious career of creative chemistry for Myron. Once I had discovered the secret of realistic looking artificial messes, he realized that the possibilities were endless. From that point on, the rest of the family couldn't pick anything up without worrying that Myron might have laced the underside of the object with something like slick, artificial boogers. His simulated vomit was convincing at first glance, although it didn't have the distinctive piquant bouquet that so often accompanies the real thing. He was a genius, whose mother of invention wasn't necessity at all. It was mere mischief.

Does it make you feel any better to know that now that he's grown up, he's in the food business?

He was also good at using his electrical set to rig up light-activated fluffer sounds. For those of you who are unfamiliar with the word "fluffer" or "passing wind," as the Victorians used to say, it is a scientific term used to describe the outward expressions of flatulence. The action was often followed by the words "bad dog" in our home. I believe the introduction of this phrase was one of my parent's doing. We don't know which one, as neither one of them will admit to it now.

Myron comes by his mischief honestly. My mother is the woman who strategically placed tiny plastic ants all over the muffins at school. She didn't dare 'fess up to it after one of the teachers declared that the muffins had to be thrown away because they were bad.

She was also the one who put a squirt of mustard in my younger sister's baby doll's diaper when my sister was asleep. She learned this trick from her own mother. We refer to it as the Mustard Legacy, and I'm sure it will be passed on for generations to come. As long as there is mustard on the store shelves, there will be traumatized posterity.

Another of my mother's famous kitchen feats involved the use of a wooden spoon. I'm not sure she ever used it on us. If she did, I have successfully blocked it out of my memory. What I remember is this short-ish woman looking like a giant ogre as she ran after us, banging that spoon on the counter as she went. The noise and the image were enough to strike fear into even Myron's heart. Forget about "Speak softly and carry a big stick." Just carry a big wooden spoon, and holler like the dickens.

My mother's favored method of punishment involved the kitchen as well. She claims she was doing the best she could, but I think she did it on purpose. It was her homemade wheat bread. It may have been smaller than a breadbox, but it weighed more than a refrigerator. And if it wasn't sliced at least three inches thick, it crumbled to pieces. Lucky us. We got peanut butter and honey on four inches of whole wheat for lunch. It wouldn't have been so difficult if we had had unhinge-able jaws. And bad as the bread was, her whole wheat snicker doodles were worse. You didn't just dunk those things in milk. Nope. You had to soak them overnight. She actually made some for me to bring to school for a party one time. I was careful to bring them in an unmarked, brown paper bag and deposit them on the table when nobody was looking.

I'm just thankful that my mom's Soap-Making Episode didn't pan out, or rather that it did. If you're gifted, you already know that gifted people often think they're too smart to stoop to the level of those who read and follow instructions. What? Don't put lye in an aluminum pan? Silly details! Who has time to worry about that kind of stuff?

That was right before she had to yell at my dad to come get the bubbling over, rapidly dissolving aluminum vat of soap-from-the-dark-side and rush it out to the yard where the damage would be limited and the stuff would only kill the grass and threaten the ecosystem.

She never attempted soap-making again. She couldn't afford another pan.

Pandora's primary kitchen accomplishment up to this date, at age four and a half, would have to do with a certain prize in a cereal box. It was a beanie toy. Now, at our house, we buy cereal on sale and by the case. This beanie toy had to be about the eleventh prize of its kind in our household. Pandora probably owned three or four of the identical toys already, but that wasn't enough. Nope. Nobody can have too many beanie toys, even if they're all the same character. Eager to get her greedy little mitts on the next toy, she asked if she could open the box of Crunchy Wunchies and get it out. Since we already had an open box of Crunchy Wunchies, and since I am a mean, heartless, and tyrannical mother, I said, "No."

Her shoulders drooped, but she said, "Okay," and went back into the kitchen to eat her breakfast.

I didn't think any more about it. When I went into the kitchen later, there she sat with one open box of Crunchy Wunchies, one closed box of Crunchy Wunchies, and a bowl full of the stuff. When she finished, I began cleaning up. I picked up and closed the first box, and placed it in the cupboard. Then I picked up the second box to place it in the cupboard as well. Only there was a slight glitch. As I picked up the box, the entire contents fell out of the bottom and onto the floor. My eyes met hers as I listened to the pitter-patter of dry cereal bits raining down around my legs and landing in a deep pile around my feet. I have no idea how I appeared to her, but to me, she appeared to be on the slightly worried side.

I looked first at the floor and then at the bottom of the box. The little twerp had cut the cardboard bottom off in a trim rectangle, had slit the inner lining, and had removed the beanie toy. Then she'd carefully placed the box on its bottom and set it back on the counter just as though it had never been touched.

The bright side is that she should have no problem with fine motor skills when they test her for kindergarten.

If houses could talk, our kitchen would have to go in for therapy.

⊞ 12: Two for the Show

Okay, let's say that you take six varieties of highly gifted, junior high brains and put them together in one room, then you give them a coach or two, an assignment, and some duct tape. What do you get?

Give up?

No, not hostages.

You get an exercise in futility. But it's an awfully entertaining way to go.

You also get an Odyssey of the Mind™ team. And believe me, this is one Odyssey that would have blown Homer right out of the water.

If you've never had an Odyssey of the Mind™ experience, well, then you should. Everyone should. Particularly people who are suffering from depression or a stress-related disorder. (You know, the sort of disorder where you wake up every morning and have to get out of bed and eat breakfast and read the paper and go to work, because Never-Never Land is a nice concept but nobody left you a map.)

Odyssey of the Mind™ is an international program to encourage creative thinking. If you want to know more about it, you can check out its official site at www.odysseyofthemind.com.

Anyway, it's highly therapeutic, working with these kids.

It's also, ironically, highly stress-inducing.

Remember the focus chapter? Try getting six chatty, unorganized, easily distracted kids to build and paint props. My main job as coach was to redirect their attention to whatever task was at hand. Then, after having managed to convince them to focus on the paint, or the paintbrush, for what seemed like five seconds, their focuses would drift into the mysterious territories of their brain lands, and I'd redirect them again.

"Harvey, you have a paintbrush in your hand, not on the ceiling."

Harvey would bring his gaze down to earth where I was sitting and he'd say, "What? Paintbrush? Oh, yeah!"

And then ten seconds later we'd repeat the process—times six.

Needless to say, I encouraged them to keep the props simple—which, since one of the kids was an engineer in embryo form, was even more difficult.

One of the challenges was to have a technical element in the skit. Now for me, blowing up a balloon without popping it is pretty technical, but for Horatio—well, for Horatio, things couldn't be technical enough.

He'd shout, "Hey, I have an idea!"

"What?" we'd all ask.

Now, in Odyssey of the Mind™, the rule is that there are no dumb ideas, just dumb coaches who are parent volunteers—suckers.

Okay, so I added that last part.

But as Horatio would explain each of his ideas for the technical element, I could feel my brain curl up like a pill bug.

He'd say, "Okay, I've got it all figured out. We'll build a box so high by so wide, see. Then we'll have a lever sticking out where no one can see it but us. The lever will be connected to about six other levers in the box, like this, and when the main lever is pushed, it'll trigger all the other levers. Eventually, the last lever will press up on a gear that will turn a wheel that'll have a rubber band around it for a belt, and that will rotate...."

And so on.

This is the same kid who, the year previous, convinced the team that they needed a pop-up background. He'd figured out how to take a fifty-four inch square cardboard box, which held all of the other props, and turn it into a fifteen foot long, six foot high backdrop. Explode-a-scenery. It was a great idea and earned some points, as it was a creative way to use the limited space allowed for props, but it was also complicated and difficult to transport—which explains why the second year, the kids rebelled on the scenery end of things and put together a much simpler, much smaller "Book o' Scenes." It was a poster board flipchart. One person could hold it, and the only moving parts involved binder rings and page turning.

I told them, "Good idea. Sometimes less is more." What I was thinking was, less is less—less hassle, less packing space, less work, less cattle prodding.

And try writing a script with six kids who can brainstorm up a level four hurricane. We spent weeks trying to get them to settle down to just one subject for their skit. "Oh yeah, yeah, let's do that one, that's good!" they'd say in unison. Gifted kids spark one another when they get together. Like fireworks. They would spend five whole minutes shouting out lines and writing them down. Then, inevitably, one of the kids would say, "Wait a minute! I've got another idea!" which would start them on another roll, only to be interrupted by another change of course, ad infinitum.

The first year's skit finally ended up being a spoof about President Clinton and an atom bomb that Saddam Hussein had disguised as a beautiful woman prior to a weapons inspection. This timely piece was written a month or two before the Lewinsky scandal broke out and was performed during the peak of the media hullabaloo. Man, what a relief when that was over—five sixth grade boys and one seventh grade girl who were always anxious to learn new things and then exercise their wit. They could have livened up their skit into one big censored bleep, but I didn't think that was the kind of creativity the judges had in mind. I ran from comment to comment and stomped out each fire as soon as I saw the sparks.

The second year, their skit was a spoof of the Boston Tea Party, combined with the witch's chant in Macbeth. I know, I know, it's a natural combination, isn't it? The two things go together like ham and cheese. The kids' assignment had been to take a moment in history, combine it with a moment from Shakespeare, and write eight minutes worth of entertainment while fitting an original song into the performance.

By that time, we'd been through a lot together. So in the second year, when our team made it to the state competition, we were thrilled.

And when they announced at the state competition that our team had qualified for the international competition in Knoxville, Tennessee, we all jumped up and screamed and hurrahed.

I jumped and screamed and hurrahed with everyone else, but the awful secret is that inside I shouted, "Oh, noooooooooooo!" Because now we had to not only keep up the practice, and rebuild the props, but we had to raise the ten thousand dollars to pay for a trip that was only two months away.

And *that* was the mother of all creative problem-solving situations.

We managed it only with a lot of help from friends, relatives, and the local folks. The really scary part was when someone or other would offer to make a contribution if the kids would work for it. This is a nice concept, but there I was with six kids who could barely remember to wiggle the paintbrush when it was on the paper. How in the world was I going to manage to get them to sweep off a sidewalk or pick up rocks?

A younger brother of one of the teammates, Rodney, was a big help. He walked up to us after an assembly at the school holding a cup full of dollar bills. He'd gone begging for our team.

After scolding him and lecturing him on the ethics of fund-raising, we quickly pocketed the money in the Odyssey of the Mind™ account and hoped he'd pull through for us again.

Two months later, we boarded the plane to Tennessee. There were three of us adults and seven children. You could tell who the adults were. They were the ones squeezing each other's hands, gasping for air, and squinching their eyes shut every time the plane took off or landed.

Knoxville was a lovely place, especially since it meant we had a full week of being grounded for the competition before we had to face the anti-gravity ordeal again.

The opening ceremonies were incredible. It was a mini-Mental Olympics, complete with flags from China, Denmark, and the Slovakian Republic, among many others. The auditorium was huge, and it was packed with G/T kids from all over the world. That was the amazing part. First, I thought about my son Stanley, who was on the team, and how weird he was. I multiplied that times six for each of the members on his team. Then I multiplied that by a few hundred, so that I could try and visualize the magnitude of weirdness that was in that building. Talk about clustering. If Elvis had been in the building at that point, he would have been running to the exit, and I wouldn't have blamed him. The world is a scary place.

We found our dorms without a hitch. It was nice to room with Madge, mother of another gifted child or two and coach for our younger team. She was the first person who, when I said, "Stanley is so smart. I just don't know what to do with him," answered, "I'm sorry. I know just how you feel."

What a relief to hear that. Previous to this moment, when I said something like this, most people looked at me as if they wanted to gag.

Madge is gifted. We had our suspicions, but she proved it when she tried to grab a roll out of a display basket of varnished bread. It's true, the food at the cafeteria wasn't all that great anyway, so a little varnish on a parker house roll, a roll that was hard enough to be used to shatter a window should a fire break out and make it necessary for us to find an emergency escape route, would hardly be noticeable.

Madge probably could have gotten by without notice if one of the servers hadn't stopped the whole line to holler loudly in a southern accent, "Uh, excuse me, ma'am, but that there's varnished bray-ed."

And the entire cafeteria crowd looked at Madge, who stood there, eyebrows up and with a frozen guilty smile on her face, a roll in her right hand and a plate in her left. And they must have thought, she's gotta be one of those Odyssey of the Mind™ people.

Odyssey of the Mind™ people, with the possible exception of Madge at that moment, love the spotlight. That's one reason gifted kids enjoy the program so much. It finally gives them a chance to be just as strange and unique as they possibly can be, and not only do they get attention, they get points for it. It's the higher-level thinking, the kind of creative stuff that often isn't allowed in classrooms, that judges are looking for.

And each of the kids is thinking, wow, cool, imagine that. Somebody actually *wants* me to be my creative and divergent self. Finally, my brain is free to roam! Every meeting is a breath of freedom for them, an opportunity to be themselves. By the time they finally get to the stage, they're primed and ready for the big time. Ahem, excuse me, all eyes on me, please.

If Stanley were ordering from the menu of life, he'd probably say, "I'll take the Spotlight Special with a little Attention on the side."

An audience is almost a necessity for him. If an adult tries to talk to him one-on-one, he can't seem to look him or her in the face. When he answers the phone, it's a deep and monotone hello. Boring. No energy.

Although Stanley may be lacking in social skills, put him on stage, give him a chance to perform in front of a large group of people, and voila! He becomes Stupendous Man! His own transformation makes the Jekyll-Hyde contrast look like the difference between night and night. He can crack jokes, he can look the audience in the eye, he can think on his feet without feeling the least bit nervous. Could somebody please increase the wattage on that spotlight? And turn up the microphone!

It's like when my friend's daughter, Stephanie, was younger and was very impressed by a three-way mirror. "Look, Mom," she said, "All of these people are looking back at me!"

However, the attention thing is a diverse thing. The spotlight shoe does not fit every child's egotistical foot in the same way.

Take Otto, for example. Otto stands tall, does well with personal conversation, thrives with individual attention, but would really prefer to avoid, thank you very much, any sort of large audience. He can speak in front of a crowd if he has to, but it isn't something he'd volunteer for.

Then there are the kids like my brother, Myron, who enjoyed getting all sorts of individual attention along with the spotlight touch. My mother used to wonder why people in all of the other cars would stare at us when they passed. She probably thought that they were impressed by her flock of well-behaved children in their matching clothing. Uh huh.

It was more likely the fact that my brother had stuffed wads of toilet paper up both nostrils and then stuck his face to his window where he would be sure to be seen. Sound typical for a little boy? Yeah? Well, how about a fifteen-year-old?

Hey, he was bored. What's a guy supposed to do, listen to the radio?

My mom was understanding though. She said that when she was five and her sister Eloise was four, Eloise was supposed to perform at a recital. However, when they announced her name, Eloise decided in that very instant, thanks anyway, but she had no desire to get up and sing in front of a large audience. My mother saw her chance. Before anyone could stop her, she ran up to the stage and belted out "Home on the Range." A five-year-old ham. It was a Little Rascals moment. Darla would have been jealous.

❁ ❁ ❁

When I was in sixth grade, I wrote a poem. I showed it to my teacher with great hopes that she would think it was just as cool as I thought it was and that she would share it with the class so they would think it was cool, too.

It worked. She read it to the class. I was so proud, I hid my head under the lid of my desk for the entire reading, cursing myself, and yet grateful that I'd written so many wonderfully brilliant lines. That's my love/hate thing with attention. I want it, but please don't look too hard at me because I can't stand the pressure.

I've mentioned previously that music was not one of my better talents, but music wasn't always a bane to me, and neither was attention. There was one time, a time when I really stood out from the maddening crowd, a time when stardom was within my grasp, a time when I found my niche, my comfort zone, my hidden spring of musical talents.

I was in a junior high musical, and miracle of miracles, I got a singing part. I had several numbers I had to perform, most of them solo, some of them duet, all of them spotlight performances. Yes, I'm not embarrassed to admit it—I was good that night. I was unstoppable. My drama teacher was proud. The audience roared. I confidently belted out every song at the top of my lungs.

I became Maggie, the drunk, dancehall girl has-been.

Sadly, there wasn't much call for off-key singers in the rest of my short-lived acting career.

Too bad they didn't have Odyssey of the Mind™ when I was younger.

Our state is no longer involved with the Odyssey of the Mind™ program, but is now using a similar program called Destination ImagiNation®. (For more information, go to www.destinationimagination.org.) Imagination is the key word here. For most gifted kids, it is the key word anywhere. It's their link to creativity and the world they live in. It's also what makes living in the normal, everyday world, an unavoidable reality, into something a little more endurable.

Take the kid who was a loner on the playground when he was in elementary school. He had a toilet paper insert that he carried around everywhere with him so he could speak into it and ask Scotty to beam him up.

My mother had the opportunity to speak into this advanced wonder of scientific technology once, but thankfully, she didn't hear any voices coming from the other side—not that she'll admit to anyway.

Imagination is what makes creative problem solving possible, because it envisions the supposedly *im*possible.

You want to know what creative problem solving is? Let me give you one real-life example. Let's just say that there is a little neighbor boy who is in your sister's first-grade class. His name is Vincent, but your mother calls him Vincent the Vegetable Vampire. He probably doesn't really care for vegetables all that much, but that is beside the point. This six-year-old Vincent kid is a pest. He comes over and knocks on your door about five or six times a day looking for your little sister, who we'll refer to as, oh, let's say her name is Edna. This gets to be rather annoying. So what do you do?

Do you take him aside the next time he rings the doorbell and tell him, "I'm sorry, but you aren't allowed to come over more than once a day, and I would recommend that you save that once a day for emergency use only"?

Do you call his mother and talk to her, hoping to solve the problem with her help, and also hoping that she's not the one sending him over because he is on the annoying side and she doesn't know what else to do with him, but she figures that her sanity is more important than yours?

Do you just not answer the door? Do you turn off the lights and pretend no one is home?

Well, let me tell you what my family did. We used creative problem solving. The next time Vincent rang the doorbell, my brother Myron answered the door.

Vincent asked, "Can Edna play?" Myron looked at Vincent as though he could not for the life of him understand a word that Vincent said. Then Myron began speaking to Vincent in Chinese. I'll not try to reconstruct the entire conversation in this book, because I don't know anything about the Chinese language—other than the words sound like ping and pong and Hong Kong and gong gee. This did not stop Myron, who knows about as much as I do about the Chinese language, from attempting to speak it to Vincent. He must have figured that the odds were in his favor that Vincent knew nothing of the language either and would be easily fooled.

Vincent wasn't easily fooled, but it turned out that he was easily puzzled. He finally gave up on getting anywhere with Myron and went home. But with his usual dogged determination, Vincent returned a few minutes later and rang the doorbell again.

This time it was my turn. I tried to emulate Myron's fine example, and I must have done so with some success, as Vincent once again gave up and went back home.

A few minutes later, he returned for one last try. And as Myron and I had exhausted our limited Chinese vocabulary, we allowed our mother the privilege of taking up where we left off while we watched the victim through the living room window.

Now, while Vincent might have expected Myron to do something like that, and while he might have been less than shocked to see me do it as well, he certainly wasn't prepared to see my, ahem, "respectable" mother answer the door and speak Chinese to him as though it were her native tongue. His mouth dropped open and he stared at my mom as she rattled away.

He left, and didn't come over again that evening. I don't remember how long it was before he did return.

You know, this is a great parenting technique to use with gifted children. Whenever they get annoying and repetitive and demanding and whiny, well, just speak to them in Chinese until they go away. Unless they *are* Chinese, of course. Then you'll have to find another foreign language or just make one up.

Anyway, so that experience, in a very large nutshell (and the word "nut" is not used lightly), is an example of creative problem solving. You look for ideas that might work, try them, evaluate, and go on.

When my sister Hortense was frustrated, she brimmed with intelligence and creative problem-solving skills. Once, when she was angry with our sister Gertrude, she felt as though she had to say something that really expressed her anger, something so bad that Gertrude would know just how serious the situation was, and something that let her know that she, Hortense, wasn't going to put up with it anymore.

Since we weren't allowed to swear, or to even use the word "stupid," Hortense got creative. She sucked in her cheeks and balled her fists and said, "You're a…you're a…a penguin sitting on a cliff!"

Words can be so hurtful. But after much evaluation, that was probably not an effective insult.

Are you ready for another fine example of imagination, this time starring my mother when she was in sixth grade? Here goes. She had a humongous crush on this kid named Lee, and she wanted a picture of him for worship purposes. Should she: (A) ask for a school photo, (B) bring a camera to school and snap one when he wasn't looking, or (C) wait for him to do something brilliant and then cut his picture out of the newspaper?

The answer was (D) none of the above. Instead, she told her mother, who was a portrait artist, that she was supposed to go over to Lee's house and paint his portrait in chalks. So her mother, innocently believing that Lee's mother had requested this and that she and Lee knew all about it and were expecting her, packed up her chalks and drove my mom and herself over to Lee's house.

Needless to say, it didn't turn out at all like my mom had planned. Lee ran away and hid even after threats of being spanked, and my mom ended up with a broken, though hardly daunted, heart and a lecture on chasing boys.

But lucky for Lee, my mom was gifted, determined, and creative. She kept trying. He must have spent the entire sixth grade living in fear.

⊞ ⊞ ⊞

My mother can be creative on her feet. I remember one Christmas Eve when I was about five and Myron and I couldn't sleep. We were told to stay in bed and listen for the sleigh bells and the reindeers' hooves on the rooftop. We waited and waited but heard nothing. Finally, we both agreed that something must have gone wrong, because it had to be almost morning by that time. So we went downstairs to see if Santa had managed to sneak in without us hearing him.

Imagine the devastation we felt when we saw our mother sitting at the kitchen table filling our stockings.

Mom looked at us, never breaking character, and said, "You two had better hurry up and get back to bed. Look, I had to crawl up on the roof to get this stuff. Santa had to leave it there because you weren't asleep yet. And he left a note asking me to take care of this for him because he didn't have time to wait. He's going to stop back by later to drop off the presents, but if you're still awake, he's just going to keep flying."

We must have fallen directly asleep after that, because I don't remember anything more except that we woke up to a wonderful and un-disillusioned Christmas morning.

Growing up with a creative mother was magical, but it was also practical. I hesitate to admit this, but my mother taught me how to sew. Or how not to sew, depending on how you look at it. That helped me make it through high school when money was scarce and I either had to save my lunch money for a full month to buy a new shirt or save for a week to buy enough fabric to make one. Granted, if you were to ask my classmates how funny my clothes looked, they would probably try to be very kind and say they can't remember. But I did make every effort to at least color coordinate things.

Fortunately, the yearbook picture is only from the neck up.

Thanks to the lessons in ingenuity that I learned from my mother, I was able to cut down my own sweaters and jeans to remake clothes for Stanley when he was two and his dad was in school and we were struggling to survive. Thankfully, Stanley was young enough that the trauma of being dressed in his mother's old castoffs is a bit beyond the realm of memory for him. But hey, he was warm. And I used matching thread.

Good thing he was too young for underwear.

Besides, a mother like me really comes in handy when Stanley wants something like fake fur pants. It's not as though they sell them at Sears.

In our school, one of the ways that they teach creative problem solving is with problem-solving kits that they've put together for the kids. They're sort of like Odyssey of the Mind™ or Destination ImagiNation® on a less grand scale. They are intended to encourage creative thinking. Nonetheless, any time my mom decides to replicate the problem at home for a family activity at, say, Thanksgiving or something, she accuses my dad and me of cheating. (Actually, I am the innocent party and it's a matter of guilt by association.) The problem arises when she only tells us what we can do, not what we can't do. My dad usually manages to solve the problem within seconds using highly questionable and unconventional methods. And I have to ask my mom, "Isn't that the point?"

She then docks us and we end up in last place.

The cool thing about creative problem solving is that every experience is different. It's just a matter of dreaming something up and putting it into practice.

❖ ❖ ❖

When I was a kid, I wanted to be a sculptor, along with about a thousand other things. But how could I become a sculptor when I didn't have access to measly stone and chisel, not even Play-Doh®, because I was banished to my room for quiet time? Simple. All I had to do was scrounge around under the bed until I found some dust-covered crayon pieces and then melt them over the light bulb in my lamp. Pretty creative, no?

So what if it left an ugly brown splotch on the top of the light bulb along with an off-smelling odor reminiscent of smoke. Hey, it was all for the sake of art. People have sacrificed a great deal for art. Any lung disease that I can attribute to the inhalation of melted crayon smoke in my youth is a small price to pay. Besides, I still have both my ears, so I figure I'm getting off easy.

Creativity is a kid's best friend. It's what got Myron and Gertrude and me through summers of bitter dandelion leaf salad when we were playing pioneers and decided to live off the land.

It's what makes it possible for three siblings under the age of eight to build an airplane out of their dad's wood scraps and really believe they can make it fly.

It's why a six-year-old boy can design in detail his own pair of wings and convince his teenage sister to make them for him out of poster board and newspaper, only to try them out while jumping on the trampoline and to discover that they don't work.

It's also why this same boy was so confident in his own thought process that he figured the only reason why they didn't work was because his sister had somehow messed up on his design.

It means that a nine-year-old boy can build an entire suit of armor out of notebook paper, right down to the pointy shoes. It means having imaginary friends like the one Otto had when he was four. Her name was Zeanna and she lived in a crack in the sidewalk. It means having whole imaginary families like Magnolia and her Rabbit family. It means seeing things that aren't there, and you know that, but it's beside the point because they are there in your brain and that's all that counts.

Imagination made it possible for Magnolia to pretend to be a dog when she was three. I know a lot of children may pretend to be dogs, but how many of them lick your feet?

I am now in the habit of wearing socks around the house.

Creativity and imagination are responsible for a lot of the unexplained mysteries of the world. When Stanley's friend, Alfred, was younger, he lived in a home on a dairy farm that was cat heaven. They were everywhere. And they spoke to Alfred in a language only he could understand. He told his parents that it was Spinish. They asked, "Don't you mean 'Spanish'?"

No, he meant "Spinish." Perhaps it was the original language of all vertebrates, but Alfred was the only human vertebrate who recognized it when he heard it. It must have been some kind of evolutionary flashback.

My imagination has always been my best friend—and probably my worst enemy, too. I don't think I have ever gone through a day when I haven't lived at least part of it in an alternate reality of some sort. I still do this as an adult, but when I was a kid, my imagination tugged on my brain during every waking hour, and often during the sleeping hours too.

I remember one instance when I was five and Myron was three, we had the upstairs of an old farmhouse all to ourselves, and I, being the morally upright and ethically correct person that I've always been, decided it would be a real thrill to scare the bejeebers out of my little brother.

So one night, I wrapped myself up in a bed sheet and hid in the closet under the eaves to await my brother, who would be coming back up at any moment from a trip to the bathroom. I had a story all made up about Count Somebody and his Frankenstein sidekick. It was great.

As soon as Myron crawled back into his bed, I creaked opened the closet door and began wailing. Slowly, I made my way to the side of his bed and proceeded to introduce myself. I disguised my voice and everything. I was no dummy.

He said, "I know it's you, Karen."

"Nooooooo! It's not me. I'm Count Somebody! If you don't believe me, then I'll have to send out Frankenstein to prove it." At which point I wailed all of the way back to the closet, did a quick change with the sheet, and returned to Myron's bedside with my arms out in front of me and my feet dragging.

Myron looked at me and yawned.

I thought, wow, he must be one smart cookie to be able to see through my disguises every time.

But the experiment wasn't a total failure, because after I crawled into my own bed that night and began thinking about it, well, who was to say there wasn't a *real* Count Somebody and a *real* Frankenstein living in our closet under the eaves.

I believe I slept with the covers over my head all that night, and never walked by that closet again without a chill of fear as I thought about the two seedy characters that lived inside of it.

Myron, however, remained unshaken. I think he was saving all his imagination for his own fantasy world.

He used to bury strings of firecrackers in the ground and tamp the dirt down so he could make an army camp. Then he'd set all his little figures up to play war and light the fuse that was poking out of the ground. Live action. No batteries required. Let me tell you, there are gender differences.

When he was eleven, he was the kid riding his dirt bike down steep hills and onto jumps improvised by using a two-by-four and big rocks, because he had enough imagination to believe that he was beyond danger.

He was also the kid with the broken arm.

He had no fear.

When I was about ten and he was eight, we used to sleep outside at night on the deck surrounded on three sides by pine trees, and we'd take turns reading out of the book *Grizzly.* We were both fully aware that a black bear had been spotted recently in the neighborhood. Myron was the only one who actually slept. I mostly stayed curled up inside my sleeping bag holding as still as I possibly could. My hope was that, with any luck, the bear would get Myron first and be full. It would also mean a freed up bedroom, which I could move into so that I wouldn't have to share with my younger sisters.

I always had a vivid and rather paranoid imagination. I can't swim in public pools because of all the floaties, whether they are actually tangible or nothing more than a sensation that there is an unseen presence, a warm one, in the water with you. I refer to the public pool as "snot soup." Call me weird, but it seems real to me. Whether it makes sense or not is beside the point.

🎴 🎴 🎴

Several rabbits that were under my care when I was a child never lived to see another summer because of one of my fears. It was my job to pick grass and feed it to them every morning, but all I could think of was the squishy feel of mashed caterpillar under my fingers every time I tried to pull up a handful of grass. I never did actually mash one, but the idea by itself was enough to make me ill. It was also enough to make me pick the grass one or two blades at a time. I was very sensitive to other living creatures, especially the ones that I was afraid of.

I'm hoping that those rabbits weren't any relation to the Rabbit family that Magnolia lived with in her other life. If they were, they probably sent her to me in an act of revenge. It would explain the food hoarding business too.

I was often haunted by the creepy things of the earth. You'd think I'd be used to worms for all the digging that I did and with a history of falling asleep to the worm song. But I was too stubborn to become desensitized. My younger sisters took advantage of this and often chased me with worm, frog, grasshopper, or caterpillar in hand until I locked myself in the bathroom and stood on the sink just in case they slipped whatever little demon it was under the door.

I'm still haunted to this day. I can't eat in the shade of a tree, because I am afraid of a caterpillar falling out of the leaves and onto my hair or into my food. I can't sit or walk barefoot on the grass because of what might be crawling in it. I struggle with sleeping on a floor, because a spider or mouse might crawl on me. And weevils? Don't even go there.

I never did fall for the old "You're bigger than they are; they're more afraid of you than you are of them" routine. Nope. I'm too smart for that.

I've heard there's therapy to help you overcome these kinds of fears. I've never understood that. Why would anyone *want* to overcome fears? I'm afraid of my fears. I want nothing to do with them. I have no desire to learn how to coddle a snake or hold a spider in the palm of my hand and pretend as if he's cute and cuddly and willing to love me back. Besides, I figure my fears are keeping me alive. They're healthy things. I mean, if I'm afraid of heights, I'll probably avoid tall buildings and high bridges and narrow ledges—less opportunity to fall to my death. True? And my fears of sharks and mountain lions are also good things for the same reason. You'll never find me in a shark tank or wandering alone on a wild mountainside, which just increases the odds by that much that I'll end up dying of old age, not death by bite.

Repeat after me, "Phobias are our friends."

But getting away from phobias and back to the productive side of imagination....

Imagination is what it takes to write an advertisement for Sea Monkeys. It also takes an imagination to cope with sending for them, growing them, and finally facing the fact that they aren't really miniature fish people who have nice smiles and live in two-parent families, and that you'll never be able to sew tiny clothes for them and dress them up or try to communicate with them in sign language.

Some things are better before the reality check.

And back to Odyssey of the Mind™ and Destination Imagi-Nation®. The only problem with the two programs is that you can compete only up to the college level. My co-coach and I worked hard to sit on our hands and bite our lips, because coaches aren't allowed to interfere with the kids' thinking processes. It has to be all their own work. Any cheating and you're disqualified.

We wanted, and even needed, our own team, an adult team. We wanted to play too! Perhaps we could get a petition going. We could use a little limelight every now and then, especially for the wild and crazy rather than respectable and mature behavior.

Maturity is usually way over-rated.

Maybe I'll start my own program. It will require participants to combine a moment in car repair history with a selection from *TV Guide* and then write an original skit without any help from their children. And the technical element can be anything from standing on a scale without it registering the correct weight to building a revolving refrigerator door.

The team will get extra points if it can answer annoying and relentless questions about car keys and allowances from the judges (a panel of teenagers), and if they can fend off bill collectors without breaking character during the performance.

Lights. Camera. Action!

13: Great Expectations

Some days, I wonder if Einstein ever wanted to grow up and become a seller of patent medicines and tonics rather than a physicist. The temptation had to be there, as it was wrapped up with fame, fortune, the fancy wagon, and all the trappings.

I think of Einstein and I get this image in my brain. No, it does not involve floofy white hair and a chalkboard full of indecipherables. Instead, I see the female version in my five-year-old niece, Minerva. She's a beautiful, brown-skinned child with deep black eyes and wavy black hair. However, as black as her eyes are, when she's thinking, they're nearly transparent, because you can almost see the gears turning behind them.

I was changing Pandora's diaper once. Wait, that's sounds bad. I changed it on more than one occasion, but what I mean to say is that one time, when I was changing her diaper, Minerva was watching the process. She looked at me and said, "She's a girl, isn't she?"

I said, "Yes," and then my mischievous side kicked in. "How could you tell?"

She flashed those eyes at me and I saw the gears spinning as quickly as ever, spurred on by panic. Obviously, she had no desire to go into the finer details of the difference between boys and girls with me. After all, Minerva is the girl who told her mother that she needed more modest clothing for her Barbie dolls. Minerva's eyeballs flitted from one corner of the room to the other as she looked for a way out of this predicament. It took five-tenths of a second before she had her answer and the gears screeched to a halt, her eyes flashing and sparking and victorious.

"Because she has a dollhouse."

That was a close shave, Minerva, and under duress too.

Perhaps Minerva could eventually make a living by entering the game show circuit. All she'd have to do is practice being fast on the buzzer.

⌗ ⌗ ⌗

My first child began life as a super-brain, and we speculated on his future. Certainly he would grow up to be someone who would make a difference in the world, someone who would astound his peers, someone who would be famous and make us rich.

Well, okay, so rock stars can do all of that, I suppose. But somehow, it isn't what I had envisioned for him.

And it gets worse. A few years ago, when these noble aspirations first arose, he was thinking big. He was going to grow up, become famous, and hopefully earn enough money to purchase his own van. Why a van? Because he could live in it too. Cool, huh? And not just any van. He had plans. He wanted red shag carpet and black and white faux-cowhide upholstery. He'd hang bead curtains between the front seats and the back.

How can I describe the pride I feel when I think of my son at the epitome of success, in his eyes, behind the wheel of a rusty van with a bobbing dog head on the dashboard?

Actually, things aren't quite that bad now. He's matured a bit since then, thank goodness. He's gotten over the van. Now he's designing his single-wide trailer.

This comes as a double blessing. First, a single-wide will probably have electricity and running water. And second, he can't drive it.

You see, Stanley has inherited his driving skills from his mother, the woman who made a left-hand turn into downtown rush hour traffic, only to discover that there was an island in the middle of the road that prevented her from crossing into the far lane, and required her to continue to drive against the traffic until an opening in the island became available. It was a little like Moses must have felt when he was parting the Red Sea. All of the traffic just sort of moved off into the other lane for me like a well-choreographed car show. So what if the drivers were cursing and swearing the whole time. I couldn't hear them. Only problem was that I had my sisters in the car with me, so I had witnesses who, afterward, were eager to share their experience with anyone who would listen. Otherwise, I wouldn't be mentioning this right now. It's not as though my reputation for safe driving, or lack thereof, needs any more shoring up.

Lucky Stanley has obviously inherited my incredible motorist skills and my superb ability to be at one with a moving vehicle. So maybe being a rock star won't be so bad. They have chauffeurs, don't they?

You know, he started off so well. I just can't understand it.

I remember when he was in first grade, he wrote a poem. It was brilliant. Excuse me, but I'm a proud parent and I want to share it with you. I have it memorized, all but the title, which was a string of names all run together.

Okay, I'm walking up to the podium and clearing my throat:

> *Mister too-long-to-write ran up,*
> *I ran down.*
> *He found a little white baby pup,*
> *I found one that was brown.*
> *He named his Rover,*
> *I named mine Scott.*
> *His got ran over,*
> *Mine did not.*
> *See what happens when your name is George?*

What did I tell you? Okay, so the subject wasn't exactly deeply philosophical. Still, the form was superb—especially for a six-year-old kid.

And now he aspires to red shag carpeting?

He used to want to be President of the United States. Okay, he wanted to become an actor first, then President, following in the footsteps of Ronald Reagan. But that was way back in sixth grade. Rock stars don't generally become presidents. Besides, the White House isn't up to Stanley's standard of living.

However, Stanley might be willing to sacrifice the rock star business if he could take over for Rowan Atkinson's Mr. Bean. Stanley went through a stage where he was Beaning every chance he had. The question "What would Mr. Bean do in this situation?" was always at the forefront of his mind. Most of the time it was okay—weird, which was normal, but okay. I did, however, have to tell him that there would be no Beaning in church. I also had to ban him from drawing caricatures of whoever was at the podium.

Actually, Stanley's perfect man is a combo of Mr. Bean and his current favorite musician, whoever that may be. It changes. He likes Ringo Starr of The Beatles. He likes Dave Matthews of The Dave Matthews Band. If Stanley could be anyone in the whole wide universe, it would probably be Weird Al Yankovic.

Stanley first began dreaming of becoming a musician when he was in seventh grade. He began putting a band together, but of course, when you put a band together, the most critical step is to come up with a profound name.

His dad suggested "The Puberties," but for some reason that his dad and I can't understand, Stanley wouldn't go for it. That was a couple of years ago, and by now the band members have changed almost as often as the name of the band. I'm now campaigning for the name "Perpetual Motion."

Otto, on the other hand (he's always on the other hand. In fact, he's even left-handed), is full of ambition. Unlike Stanley, he has no idea what he wants to be when he grows up, but I do believe it may actually involve a college education, even if he does claim to want to drop out of school right now.

This is a step up from a few years ago. He was about eight. I was canning peaches, and knowing that he was my best worker at the time, I asked him to help me. I put him to work scalding peaches so that I could peel them, and he scalded with gusto, if such a thing is possible. About halfway through the day, he piped up, "Mom, thanks for letting me help you."

Now, I'm not used to hearing a phrase like that come out of one of *my* children's mouths, but since no one was around to catch me in a faint, I held myself together and asked him, "Why?"

"Well," he said, real thoughtful-like, "when I grow up and my wife is at work, I'm going to need to know how to do all this stuff."

"Oh." Great. My son had no plans for his future other than marrying a woman with a job.

Otto is also the child who has had house plans drawn up for an addition on to the back of our home. He was planning on living there when he grew up. So needless to say, any demonstration of ambition on his part is welcomed and encouraged.

And even though Otto is the logical one, he can also be the most gullible one as well. So maybe he shouldn't grow up to be a judge, a probation officer, or a professional who administers lie-detector tests. Everyone would be telling the truth, no matter how far-fetched the story was. Everyone except for Magnolia, that is.

Otto came home one day when he was in sixth grade. He'd been on a fieldtrip with other kids from the G/T program. This clustering business is always a scary thing. Oh, sure, I'm in favor of it most of the time, but…okay, I'll just tell the story and you'll see what I mean.

Otto came home one day all excited. "Guess what, Mom!" he said.

"What, dear?"

"Rodney's brother can turn his eyeballs all of the way around to the back of his head."

"Oh, really?"

"Yeah, and if he had those special kinds of contacts, you know, the kind that light up, he could see right into his brain!"

"That's very cool," I said, "but it sounds a bit on the far side."

"No! It's all true. In fact, Rodney says that doctors are studying his brother right now, because if they can find out how he does it, maybe they can train other people to do it too. And then people could see if there was something wrong with their brains, like tumors and stuff, and doctors wouldn't have to cut them open to look."

I looked at Otto and he had that look in his eyes, the earnest look, the kind of look you'd see in someone's face just before he enthusiastically wrote you out a check for that infamous Brooklyn Bridge.

Okay, so how do I break it to him that he's been had again?

It turns out that Otto wasn't the only victim. Rodney, another gifted kid who had been riding the bus with Otto, was an innocent messenger, sort of like a carrier pigeon with a flair for words. Apparently, his very gifted older brother or one of his friends had been the original author of the story, and it was too impressive for Rodney not to believe and pass on.

Maybe Otto should stick with peaches. And his wife should never let him have the checkbook.

🏵 🏵 🏵

Magnolia knows just what she wants to be when she grows up. She's going to be a school teacher. School teachers are nice, and they are loved and idolized by their students. They give out really neat pencils on Valentine's Day. They *get* gifts from almost every student in the class at Christmas and at the end of the year. These are not small considerations. Besides, teachers get to dress up for work. Magnolia loves to dress up.

Schoolwork? Homework? College? Those are mere trivialities that life throws in the way to attempt to keep a person from succeeding. Except maybe college isn't so bad because of the social life that goes along with it. But as far as Magnolia is concerned, worksheets and report cards are like Brussels sprouts and spinach; nobody likes them, and their rightful place is in the garden—as compost.

I believe Pandora is going to grow up to be a doctor, or maybe a coroner. She likes to talk about red and white blood cells and epidermises. She made a series of drawings the other day, three of them to be exact, and they were numbered. The drawings were well done, but the numbers were backwards. The first drawing was a picture of a human body with the circulatory system inside of it. The second was a picture of a human body with the skeletal system inside of it. The third was a drawing of a woman's body, with an egg-shaped uterus and a cute little smiling baby inside of it. The baby was up to its neck in water.

She knows about the water because she watched *The Coneheads*, and the part where Jane Curtin's water breaks and floods their shack was very impressive to Pandora. She's not that picky about where she gets her information, as long as she gets it. So who knows, maybe she'll grow up to be a doctor of alientology. She'll specialize.

Whatever Pandora grows up to be, I just hope she's working for the good guys. She's a terrible force to reckon with when she's opposed. She's locked me out of the house on more than one occasion. My only way to get back in the house is to alternate bribes and threats until I hit on something she cares about.

But she's determined. She'll say, "Mother, my word is my bond."

I have no idea what Rupert will be. Whatever it is will no doubt involve muscles and growling. I'm going to try to steer him away from the WWF. Sort of like Sleeping Beauty's father, I'll command that all feather boas, rather than spinning wheels, be hidden or destroyed. But then he's awfully good at sandwich sculpturing as well. He eats his sandwiches into shapes and says, "Look, Mom…moon." He's also successfully created cars, guns, dogs, and people. If he ends up being serious about the sculpting business, I hope he switches mediums, because peanut butter and honey could get really messy when he carries them around in his portfolio.

I guess it really is too early to tell what career paths my children will take. Thank goodness.

Stanley may grow up to be a band teacher with a backstage pass to the faculty lounge. There's not much money in that and the wardrobe isn't necessarily any better, but the hours aren't so bad.

And he can still live in a van if he wants to. Or maybe he can remodel an old school bus.

I try to tell him that he does need to have a Plan B, just in case Plan A turns out to be a sour note. I say to him, "Do you have any idea how many gifted teenage boys plan on becoming rock stars?"

"Nope."

"Lots."

"But I'm different," he'll say.

"That's funny. That's what all of the other gifted teenage boys say too."

"Yeah, but I *am* different."

And I'll say, "Well, maybe you are, but just in case, don't you think you ought to get some good grades in school so you can get a college education? A little something to fall back on? You might lose your voice or get carpal tunnel syndrome in your guitar playing hands."

"Okay," he'll say.

"Okay" is his way of saying, "Yeah, sure, whatever makes you happy, Mom."

He has been getting a little more ambitious lately as college brochures addressed to him arrive in our mailbox. He smiles. "They want me."

I've tried to encourage him by taking him to presentations from universities, and I do know that he's planning on going somewhere. It's just a matter of convincing him that picking a college isn't enough. He's going to have to pay for it too. And good grades go a long way on the scholarship application.

I also want to help get him beyond the dream stage as far as careers go. He's going to have to choose a major eventually, and I don't know how many colleges offer degrees in "rock stardom."

Somehow, I have to get Stanley to look at his options. Is he going to be like me and set his sights on something glamorous rather than satisfying and then regret the wasted time years later? With his limited life experience, does he really know what he wants to do now?

It's important for gifted children to be exposed to as many choices as possible. They often have strong interests or obsessions and don't realize that those can be utilized in an endless variety of ways and in combination with other things that they enjoy. Instead, they may focus only on the more obvious professions and thus limit themselves.

Either that or their interests are so varied that they can't decide what they want to do. They're afraid to commit to just one future. Sometimes they'll go through college for years before they quit changing majors and find their niche.

If they can explore more options sooner, perhaps through job shadowing, internships, or researching a day in the life of whomever, then they will be more likely to be comfortable, confident, and realistic when it comes to choosing and pursuing a career.

That career may not necessarily include college, but is it too much to ask that my kids get a college education sort of as a just-in-case thing? I mean, look at me; I did. I majored for one year in Fashion Merchandising. For homework, I went shopping. For one assignment, I made a paper doll with a budget and a wardrobe of designer clothes.

Yes, it was a very difficult time in my life.

Of course, I did have to take a few general classes like Economics and English, but I didn't sweat over those. Grammar is for conformists, right? I mean, who'd have ever thought I'd need it?

So since college played such a pivotal role in my life, I'm going to do everything I can to make sure that my children have the same opportunity.

Now that I think about it, maybe Stanley's van isn't such a bad idea after all. It's got to be less expensive than a dorm.

14: Weird Can Be Beautiful

My young friend Mildred was thrilled when she found a key chain that said, "I'm not weird, I'm gifted." See? If you won't take her word for it, just ask her key chain. She's certified.

It seems as though gifted kids, or even adults, have an intense desire to be accepted as normal, while at the same time, there is an intense fear of actually being normal. It's as if they're saying, "Hey, I want to fit in, but please, I don't want to be like everyone else. I want to keep on being who I am." The trick is to help them fit in *because* they're different, not in spite of it.

Somehow, they have to find and accept the beauty in their weirdness and then remain confident in what they have to offer, whether or not the rest of society recognizes that same beauty. It's like being a Picasso in a room full of Rembrandts.

Take my mom. She works at school with a lot of intelligent, law abiding, rule abiding, well-trained professionals. They go to work every day, complete their lesson plans, follow the schedules, follow the textbooks, and teach to the standards.

Enter Mom. And she's entering in bunny ears or a big red nose. Is she trying to get attention? Well, obviously she isn't avoiding it, but mostly she's trying to shake things up a bit. It's torturous for her to do the same thing day after day. It's boring for her. And so, since she wants to avoid that which is torturous for her, she decides to have a little fun either by spoofing or torturing others—which is why my two younger sisters, who were still in high school when my mom began working at the elementary school which is on the same campus, lived in perpetual fear of the unknown and the unexpected.

Actually, Hortense had the worst of it, as she was the youngest and most easily humiliated. Edna was the girl with the mohawk, so very little embarrassed her. But Hortense was the cute blonde who wanted to appear as normal as possible, if that wasn't too much to ask.

She ran and hid when my mom tried to pick her up from junior high one day. Why? Because it's humiliating for a kid to have her female parent, a fully grown adult woman, show up at school wearing elephant ear muffs—the hind end for the left ear, and the trunk side for the right ear. You've heard of Elephant Man? Meet his understudy.

But at least back then, Hortense could run and hide, and she took full advantage of that opportunity. Unfortunately, a few years later, when she was sitting in a high school class, there was nothing to do but hide her head on her desk and cringe into oblivion.

It was Christmas time. Hortense was in biology class, and she, like every other student, heard the tinkling of bells in the hallway. She had no idea that lurking around the corner was the Personal Humiliation Zone.

My mother's eyes peeked into the doorway. It was just a scanning glance to see if her prey was trapped and helpless. Then, when she saw Hortense sitting there, my mom grinned—something reminiscent of a Grinch grin, but with a touch of innocence.

And Hortense knew she was doomed.

My mom pranced, *pranced*, into the room. She was outfitted in a pair of wings and the required halo, and she was waving a candy bar around.

"This is for my baby," she said. She handed Hortense the candy bar, turned, and pranced back out.

"Hortense, was that your mom?"

"Who? Oh, her? Nope. Never met the woman."

Okay, so you want to know why my mother has never been carried off by some nice young men in clean white coats? We have often asked ourselves that very same question. This story also might explain why my sister Hortense struggled in school at times. She had to spend most of her class time with her face hidden and her head on her desk.

She also had to wake up some mornings to the sounds of footsteps overhead, as she heard my dad chasing my mom around the house while my mom screamed, "Harold, no, no!" My dad thought it was funny to catch her and kiss her without his dentures in his mouth. Pucker up, babe. If you ever do get a chance to meet my dad, ask to take his teeth out and smile for you. That's the *real* him.

Fortunately for my sister, she is a survivor. But no matter how normal she appears, don't let her fool you. She has her own interesting quirks.

We're talking about the girl who, when she was thirteen and her friends weren't looking, walked around with a Nerf ® Hoop attached to her forehead with a suction cup. She would toss the foam ball up and try for two points. Her arms weren't long enough to go for a three pointer.

Warning: do not try this at home. My sister Gertrude, who is four years younger than I, decided to give it a try and had the suction cup on her forehead for maybe thirty seconds. Unfortunately, it left a perfectly round three-inch hickie on her forehead that was such a deep red that several layers of makeup and powder and even the combing down of bangs couldn't cover it up. It was really too bad, because that same night, she had to go meet her future in-laws for the first time.

"Danger! Gifted Future Daughter-In-Law!" It was written all over her forehead.

Remember *The Munsters*? They were a wacky family of very nice but very strange monsters. They had one normal daughter named Marilyn. I have often felt like Marilyn. But if you asked any one of my other siblings, each one would claim the title of

"Normal," except maybe for Myron, who has his pride. The thing is, I know the truth. I am the only true Marilyn in the family, minus the blonde hair.

If I appear to be weird, it's not me, it's the company that I keep. And if you don't believe me, you can just ask the neighbors.

Ask them about the time we got a trampoline and put it in our front yard. Our neighbors used to slow down and cause traffic jams just to watch my mom jump on the thing. She looked like a bird that couldn't get off the ground. Lots of arm flapping, but no air space between her feet and the fabric. She wasn't physically talented.

When she ran, she looked as though she had a football under one arm, and was blocking with the other, while her head was down and forward so she could barrel through any obstacles that were foolish enough to stand in her way.

I guess I don't have that much room to talk though, because I hear that when I run, I look more like a pair of scissors than anything. It's not as if I were ever the first one picked for any kind of athletic team game. In fact, in high school, we had to do these gymnastic routines—you know, somersaults, handstands, cartwheels, round-offs. Our teacher was a stickler on this—no excuses, everyone had to do it, all of it. That was until she saw me off practicing a headstand in a corner; I'm sure it was a dark corner where I was hoping that no one would see me. I believe my neck was at an odd angle and my feet were dangling somewhere above my ears. She came up to me and said, "Uh, Karen? You don't have to do that part, okay? And, uh, maybe skip the cartwheels and round-offs, too." I ended up doing an entire routine using only forward and backward somersaults, with much style and grace, I'm sure, and the school gratefully avoided any paramedics, sirens, or headlines.

Personally I prefer games such as three-legged soccer. I want to make sure we level the playing field by making everyone else just as clumsy as I am.

My mother was also known as the blue slug. When she was camping, she slept in a shiny blue sleeping bag. In the morning, she would roll over the top of my sisters and call out, "Steamroller!"

This technique came in handy when my grandfather, her father, was almost bedridden and had lost his will to get up.

She warned him. If he didn't get out of bed, why, she would lay down next to him and steamroll over the top of him. He didn't believe her. He should have known better. She steamrolled him all right, and he ended up laughing so hard that he forgot to be obstinate.

Now, how many nurses would think to solve the problem that way?

My sister Edna, the one who had the mohawk when she was in high school, is a fine example of weird yet beautiful. She never colored in the lines and never cared. While others might use magenta hair as a way to make a statement to prove that they are different and therefore superior to the rest of the sheep, Edna isn't like that. At least not now that she has overcome the mohawk stage. No, she's truly an artist. To her, magenta hair is beautiful whether anyone else has it or even if everyone else has it.

And my nephew, Bubba, is another example. He's only four. He's also Batman. Now, I know lots of four-year-old boys who think they're Batman, but this guy lives the part. The last time that I saw him, it was at my sister's house. He walked in the door and, with a dramatic pause, stood erect and stiff. He then continued walking slowly, silently, and with deliberation. He spoke to no one. He wore the face mask and the tall pointy bat ears, as well as the arm gear, and he wore all of this over his Batman pajamas. It's my guess that the red Spiderman underwear worn over the top of the pajamas was added for a touch of color. Being Batman does not mean that one has no fashion sense.

I said, "Hey, Bubba!"

He glanced in my direction and condescendingly acknowledged my presence without cracking a smile or breaking character.

Batman lives. Next year he'll go to kindergarten—that is, if they'll take him after they find out about the five-gallon tub of peanut butter that he and his twin sister Katie smeared all over the kitchen cupboards, floor, and the living room carpet. That was even worse than the time they filled both of my sister's tennis shoes with orange juice and then turned her watch into a submarine. Twins. That means gifted times two. Cohorts.

Thank goodness the public schools only require proof of vaccination. If they asked for behavior disclosures before they admitted children, half of my family members would be denied school entrance.

Then there's my brother-in-law, the father of Batman Bubba, who keeps hundreds upon hundreds of pens in a plastic tub under his bed. It's his pen collection. He gathers them from every corner of the earth. No writing utensil is safe if Elmer is in the vicinity. I can picture him sitting on the floor beside his bed, laughing madly as he runs his hands through the stash of pens, and lets them fall between his fingers. "They're mine. They're all mine!" Go ahead, somebody try and convince me that this is normal behavior.

Weird is the way Stanley holds his fork when he eats. We can dress him up, and we can take him out. We just can't sit by him in a restaurant.

Weird but beautiful people are the reason why movies such as *Attack of the Killer Tomatoes* are still available on video.

I believe Stanley would like to make a sequel, *Killer Tomatoes Strike Back*. Every now and then, he sits down to write. I'll read his stuff and say, "You know, this is good, but I think you should try writing something serious sometime. It will stretch you a bit."

He'll look at me as if to say, "Death first."

I've tried to assure my kids that weird is okay. It's even good, when it's done right. This doesn't mean that they have to go out of their way to scream originality. It means that they have permission to be different.

Different means that a person has the capability to look at things from an angle that escapes the traditional thinker. I remember reading in *My Friend Flicka* where the mom explained this to the dad. She told him that their son didn't look at a picture the way that other people did. Instead, he saw around the edges of the picture and all the possibilities of the beyond.

Weird is a three-year-old boy named Ulysses, whose favorite color is black. Now, myself, I love black. It's slimming, especially when I am wearing black from head to toe and all of the lights are off. But I also like other colors and would recommend them highly for certain situations. For example, black toilet paper just doesn't seem right. And when it comes to toast, I believe I'd much prefer a nice golden brown.

I taught Ulysses in a Sunday school class. His was a very serious little brain. Even before he approached his first birthday, he was a serious kid. Imagine a pre-toddler that refuses to smile at you no matter what you do or how stupid you make yourself look. His only response was to confirm the fact that, indeed, you did look stupid.

On Mother's Day weekend, I brought construction paper and markers and helped the kids in the class to cut out hearts to make cards for their mothers. I asked this young man what color he wanted his heart to be.

"Black," he said.

"Black? Are you sure? The writing won't show up on black. How about purple?"

"I want black."

"Okay." I cut out the black heart and hoped that his mother would realize that it wasn't my idea and that there was no implication intended on my part. Fortunately, she'd had previous experience and realized that from him, a black heart was a good thing. In fact, her other two older children had both gone through the same phase.

We discussed the wonder of our bodies in this same class. This is dangerous territory, I realize, and I did ask the loaded question, "Can anyone name a part of their body?" Luckily, we avoided the more controversial parts, and the kids came up with words such as "nose" and "elbow."

Except for Ulysses. He said, "Intestines, blood, bones." This is advanced stuff for a three-year-old.

I then took out my handy-dandy pad of construction paper and some scissors and made paper dolls. I dressed them to order. One little girl wanted a yellow dress, red hair, and pink shoes. Very reasonable. Then I got to Ulysses and asked him what he would like.

"What color of a shirt would you like me to make?"

"Black." Keep in mind that every word that comes out of this mouth is uttered in complete austerity.

"Okay, what color pants?"

"Black."

"Shoes?"

"No shoes."

"How about hair?"

"No hair."

"All right then. You choose a crayon to draw a face if you would like."

"No face."

So I hand him a paper doll that looks like the backside of a bald karate master.

And in his own quiet, somber way, Ulysses was thrilled.

Weird means having a creative brain, an imagination that refuses to color in the lines. It means that you can look in your daughter's dollhouse and find that she is using feminine hygiene products as Barbie pillows.

Or you look in her room one day to discover that she has decorated her walls by peeling the backs off and sticking the things up in a nicely choreographed design. Padded walls. And yes, the entire package.

Such is life.

Weird is when a cub scout makes a cake for a cake auction and the theme is boats, but while every other kid makes a pirate ship, the gifted kid makes a garbage scow, detailed right down to the garbage, and then proceeds to explain to everybody everything they ever wanted to know, or didn't want to know, about garbage scows.

Weird also means having a sense of humor, like my friend whose pregnant bellybutton poked out so far it reminded her of a nose. When it was time to go to the doctor, she took a magic marker and drew eyes and a mouth on her belly so that the nose wouldn't be lonely there all by itself.

Weird is when a kid can eat her former pet and best friend, a goat named "Chuck," and think it's really cool because her dad tells her they are Chuck steaks. Word-plays win out every time.

When I was a kid and we lived in The Boonies, it was a tradition every year at Christmastime for my dad to take us kids up into the hills so we could pick a tree for him to cut down. Our standards were strict—we would walk as far as we could; then, when we got tired or bored, we would point to the closest tree and say, "That's the one! It's perfect!" We didn't care if it *did* have only three branches and all on the same side.

So what if my dad had to use fishing line to attach the tree to a hook in the ceiling so the tree wouldn't fall over every time someone entered the tree vicinity.

And whoop-dee-doo if all of the decorations were glitter-covered egg-carton bells and crooked popsicle-stick stars, and the diverse strings of lights weighed more than the tree did. It was still a cool tree.

Now that I'm all grown up and have some sense of aesthetics, I have a nice tree. It's normal. It's pretty. It's exquisitely decorated.

It's also boring.

Weird is beautiful.

Weird is also sometimes difficult.

I have been embarrassed by my family and by my children. I have cried both because of and on behalf of my siblings and my children and myself. This giftedness business is sometimes just one more complication in an already over-complicated world of growing up, and with any luck, growing old. But this same wonderful giftedness and these same odd, quirky people have been the high points and the strong points and the never-to-be-forgotten points in my life, and I think I'll keep them all, thank you very much.

My dad has been a tease, but he has also been an anchor. My mother has been a nut, but she has also shown me the fun stuff that life can be made of—the really, really good, even if it's socially unacceptable good stuff.

When my mother found out that she was gifted, she cried with relief—relief to know that she was okay, even if she was different. My grandmother said that when my mother told her about that experience, my grandmother cried, too. Only she said her crying was from the shame, the shame of not having been astute enough or aware enough of her children to recognize what that thing was that made her children so different.

My grandmother was a schoolteacher and has always been a very unique, intelligent, creative person. There is no doubt in my mind that she, too, is intellectually and creatively gifted. She was the perfect mother for the strange and wonderful children she gave birth to. But she knew there was that need for recognition of the gifts that her children were born with, and she couldn't give it a name until finally my mother realized that, for lack of a better word, it was called plain old "giftedness" and not plain old "odd."

I told Stanley one time, "You know, you're really very weird." He said, "Yeah, I know."

"I hope you also know that I think weird is really cool, and I'm glad that you are the way you are," I said.

He said, "Yeah, I know that, too."

It hit me then that my biggest, most important role as the mom of junior brains in progress is to let each one of them know that it is okay with me for him or her to be just exactly who he or she was meant to be.

Even if it means becoming a rock star.

Just don't remind me about the van.

About the Author

Karen Isaacson has spent her entire life surrounded by talented and artistic siblings, parents, and grandparents, and some of their talent may have rubbed off. She finds time to write in between soccer games, band and choir concerts, drama practices, naps, and checking to make sure that her daughter's iguana hasn't escaped and is running loose around the house again. She currently lives in the beautiful wilds of Montana with her husband and five children.

Other Humor Books
From Great Potential Press

Off Hours
By Jean Watts, M.A.

Jean Watts presents 180 original cartoons featuring humorous views on teaching, parenting, and life in general. Busy moms and teachers will relate to these comical drawings about the stresses, worries, frustrations, and ironies they experience every day. Cartoons are reproducible for uses in teaching.
ISBN 0-910707-20-0/ 184 pages/ paperback/ $10.00

In Search of Perspective
By Jean Watts, M.A.

Jean Watts searches for perspective on her full-time jobs parenting and teaching gifted children. Her cartoon drawings present amusing viewpoints and thought-provoking insights into life with a precocious child. Drawings are reproducible for uses in teaching.
ISBN 0-910707-14-6/ 156 pages/ paperback/ $10.00

To order or to request a free catalog, contact:

Great Potential Press
P.O. Box 5057 Scottsdale, AZ 85261
Toll-free 1.877.954.4200 Fax 602.954.0185
info@giftedbooks.com
www.giftedbooks.com

Books About Gifted Children From Great Potential Press

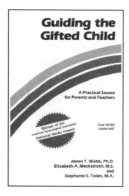

Guiding the Gifted Child
By James T. Webb, Ph.D., Elizabeth A. Meckstroth, M.S.W., and Stephanie S. Tolan, M.A.

Over 100,000 copies sold!

Called the Dr. Spock book for parents of gifted children, this award-winning book covers important information on the unique social and emotional concerns regarding gifted children. Chapters focus on motivation, discipline, relationships, stress, and depression.
ISBN 0-910707-00-6/ 266 pages/ paperback/ $18.00

Helping Gifted Children Soar
By Carol Strip, Ph.D., and Gretchen Hirsch

Also available in Spanish!

This user-friendly guidebook educates parents and teachers about gifted issues such as working together, choosing curriculum, meeting emotional needs, and finding support. A must-read to establish a solid foundation for gifted education.
ISBN 0-910707-41-3/ 288 pages/ paperback/ $18.00

To order or to request a free catalog, contact:

Great Potential Press
P.O. Box 5057 Scottsdale, AZ 85261
Toll-free 1.877.954.4200 Fax 602.954.0185
info@giftedbooks.com
www.giftedbooks.com